Young Adults with Special Needs

Assessment, Law and Practice – Caught in the Acts

of related interest

Children with Special Needs
Assessment, Law and Practice – Caught in the Acts 3rd edition
John Friel
ISBN 1-85302-280-2

Young Adults with Special Needs

Assessment, Law and Practice – Caught in the Acts

John Friel

Jessica Kingsley Publishers
London and Bristol, Pennsylvania

First published in the United Kingdom in 1995 by
Jessica Kingsley Publishers Ltd
116 Pentonville Road
London N1 9JB, England
and
1900 Frost Road, Suite 101
Bristol, PA 19007, U S A

Copyright © 1995 John Friel

Library of Congress Cataloging in Publication Data
A CIP catalogue record for this book is available
from the Library of Congress

British Library Cataloguing in Publication Data
Friel, John
Young Adults with Special Needs:
Assessment, Law and Practice – Caught in
the Acts
I. Title
362.4

ISBN 1-85302-231-4

Printed and bound in Great Britain by
Biddles Ltd, Guildford and King's Lynn

Contents

Introduction 1

1. Preparing to Leave School or Return to Further
and Higher Education Having Left School 5

2. How to Prepare the Case 15

3. Annual Reviews and Their Importance
Under the 1992 Education Act 21

4. The Nature of the Duty Under the 1992 Act 36

5. Remedies and Judicial Review 47

6. The Remaining Relevant Duties of the LEA 52

7. Transport to School or College 54

8. Other Assessments That Can Help 58

Appendix 1 – Further and Higher Education Act 1992 67

Appendix 2 – DFE Circular 1/93, 5 January 1993: The Further
and Higher Education Act 1992 Relevant Ectrants 74

Appendix 3 – Extract Code of Practice 1993 Education Act 85

Appendix 4 – Reviews: 1993 Statutory Instrument No 1047 95

Appendix 5 – Disabled Persons (Services, Consultation
and Representation) Act 1986: Extracts 102

Appendix 6 – Circular to Local Authorities, January 1988 107

Appendix 7 – Local Authority Circular, March 1993 114

Appendix 8 – Circular: Students with Learning Difficulties and/or
Disabilities by the Further Education Funding Council 117

Appendix 9 – Charities and Voluntary Organisations 130

Appendix 10 – Government Departments and Other Official Bodies 137

Introduction

The second edition of *Children with Special Needs* went to press at the time the Further and Higher Education Act was about to be passed by Parliament, and made only a very small reference to that Act. Appendix 8 of that book set out the relevant sections of the Act; the book itself provided no guide to the new statutory system. The 1992 Act represents a considerable change on leaving school. In reality, the old law covered special needs in school, and gave few rights to those who left.

It was not common knowledge among parents that the local education authority's (LEA's) duty to educate young persons continued until the age of 19 by virtue of the 1944 Education Act. The 1944 Education Act itself and the 1981 Act did not fully extend to LEAs the statutory duty to help with special·needs into post-16 further education, although they were responsible for further education. Section 41 of the 1944 Act was eventually amended and made some attempt to interlink with the 1981 Education Act, but that attempt was rather feeble.

Essentially, therefore, there existed a situation where young person with considerable problems could technically be left 'high and dry' once they came to leave school. Those who had enjoyed the protection of a statement – a minority – and those with more severe needs but no statement could find themselves without any help at all in further education.

If their parents disagreed with the help offered – if any was offered – saying it was not enough, there existed virtually no mechanism or means of getting proper help, or resolving disputes.

The 1992 Act does not create a similar appeal system to the 1981 Act or the new 1993 system. It does create clear statutory rights, where virtually none existed before. It is therefore a considerable advance from virtually nothing. Equally, the Code of Practice published under Section 157 of the 1993 Education Act is a considerable help to those transferring into further or higher education. For the parents or the young adult seeking to obtain help for their special needs in further and higher education, the key to the new system is therefore to make full preparation well in advance of the request for assistance from the further education body. The Code of Practice adopts the same approach, issued under Section 157 of the 1993 Education Act when dealing with transfer from school.

In my experience of advising in cases of children with special needs, and my knowledge of other parents' problems in dealing with similar issues, the major difficulty of which I am aware is that in many cases people need to know where to get professional advice and where to get help in order to prepare and properly present the case. Indeed, in some cases they need advice to find out what should be the future for the young person.

For that reason the book contains additional information in Appendix 9. A list of charities is included; these can provide advice and information. I apologise in advance to those charities we have not mentioned. Any advisor who believes that their organisation should be included is most welcome to write and we will endeavour to include the organisation in future editions.

As this is a book on young persons with special needs in further education, it will obviously not try to consider those legal rights which can apply in general and which can affect young persons with special needs. However, I have endeavoured to consider some associated legislation of importance: obviously, the Further and Higher Education Act in life does not stand alone.

The Chronically Sick and Disabled Persons Act 1970, the Disabled Persons (Services, Consultation and Representation) Act 1986, the Mental Health Act 1983, the National Health Service and Community Care Act 1990 and the Children Act 1989 are all relevant to the practical situation of a young person with special educational needs. Obviously, there are many other circulars and regulations. I have tried to consider or include those which are most important in this area. A great deal has been written about matters in general, but little has been done from the point of view of an individual seeking to enforce their right to have their needs met in education.

Nonetheless, the 1992 Further and Higher Education Act and the 1993 Education Act have represented considerable progress for children and young persons with special needs, and they have increased the statutory rights and protection given in this area. What is now more than clear is that there is an enormous and unjustified imbalance in the rights of young persons as opposed to children with special needs.

In the case of a young person who remains in a school, a statement continues until the young person is 19 years old or until they leave, whichever is the sooner. It is now often a matter of luck, depending on whether the local education authority has many schools with sixth forms left or only a few, which decides who will be entitled to the considerable protection of a statement, which includes appeal rights until the age of 19. No similar system of protection exists in further and higher education.

It is noticeable that the rights protecting children with special needs have expanded steadily in the last 14 years, and that extension has eventually benefited young adults with special needs. It is to be hoped that the protection of the 1993 Education Act is extended to young persons with special needs, so they are granted similar rights of appeal and protection as those given to those young persons who remain with the local education authority.

The Further and Higher Education Funding Council in its issued Circulars (some two to date), has set up a system, considered later in the book, to compensate for the lack of assessment rights, and obligations under the 1992 Act. The system is largely dependent on the active co-operation of the LEA, and upon the LEA acting within the suggested time limits.

Despite the existence of the 1986 Act, 1970 Act, and the other social services legislation, it is noticeable that the Further Education Funding Council (FEFC) has, in effect, set up its own system. The present system set up by the FEFC recognises that there will be exceptional cases, or cases where there is not agreement between parents and LEAs.

Preparing to Leave School or Return to Further and Higher Education Having Left School

For those young persons who have not left school, the first question to be asked is whether the LEA responsible for the young person is in fact carrying out its duty. For young people with statements who remain in school after the age of 16, LEAs remain under a duty to provide for them in accordance with their statements. This means that the LEA is required to fund a place for an individual in an independent special school, if his or her statement specifies that form of provision. For those in a local sixth form special school or unit, the same applies. However, if there is no reason to leave school, a young person with special needs should seek to stay there and compel the LEA to continue to be responsible for their education. This may require an amendment to the statement in appropriate cases.

In practice, some local education authorities retain few sixth forms, or young persons with statements may be placed at independent specialist schools which themselves only provide until 16. In these circumstances, a young person in a specialist school which finishes at the age of 16 is in exactly the same position as a young person whose local education authority provision in its area only extends to an appropriate school up to the age of 16. Section 4 of the 1981 Education Act, is to be replaced by Section 165 of the 1993 Act which is in much the same form, which provides that the local education authorities are responsible for a child (which includes young person), if he or she is in their area or if they have taken over responsibility for him or her under the 1993 Act. The fact that a young person has reached the age of 16 is not on its own an adequate reason for declining responsibility for their education or withdrawing a statement. Paragraph 73 of DFE Circular 1/93 makes it clear that there is a continuing requirement for LEAs to fund a place for an individual over the age of 16 who remains at school (see Appendix 2).

Many young persons within the area of an LEA receiving special educational provision, may well have considerable learning difficulties although no statement. Again, if the school continues to the sixth form, the position is that the school – therefore the LEA – retains overall responsibility for the young person's education, but not if they cease to be registered as a pupil at school. The LEA's duty ceases.

Although, therefore, the duty is placed upon the LEA to make the arrangements for a statement of special educational needs up to the age of 19, unless they decide to cease to maintain the statement, the duty is dependant on the statutory provisions. These are contained in Section 165 of the 1993 Education Act.

If the local education authority continues to exercise its statutory powers, it must, under the Act, be responsible for the young person. That requires the young person to be:

1. Registered at a maintained, grant-maintained school or special school.

2. Provided with education at a school at the expense of the local education authority which normally means an independent school.

3. Registered at a school, and having been brought to the authority's attention as having or probably having special educational needs. In this case, he will obviously require a statement, however old he is, until he reaches the age of 19. This statutory provision is intended to deal with young persons who have not been detected.

4. Not a registered pupil at a school and not under the age of two, or over sixteen. This normally applies to those children who have either been excluded from school or who have been educated at home. This category of pupil must not be over the age for compulsory schooling.

For those parents whose children attend schools which take pupils over the age of 16, it is important to ensure that, if they require the LEA to continue responsibility for the young person, the LEA is presented with a request to amend the statement in appropriate terms, or the duty to maintain the statement will cease when the young person leaves school and registration at school no longer exists. It is obviously different if the young person is in a school which goes up to the age of 19; then the same problems simply do not apply.

Although unusual, it is not at all impossible that a young person with special needs who remains at school post-16 could be entitled to a statutory assessment or, more likely, a reconsideration of their statement. For guidance as to the principles on these issues see the companion volume, *Children with Special Needs, third edition*. This deals with local education authority duties.

YOUNG PERSONS LEAVING LOCAL SCHOOLS

The 1992 Act establishes new Further Education Funding Councils (FEFCs) which, with effect from 1 April 1993, took over from LEAs their statutory duty in respect of the provision of full-time education for those aged 16–18 (see Appendix 1). The councils also took over duties in respect of part-time education for those over compulsory school age and full time education for those aged 19 and over, falling within Schedule 2 of the Act (see Appendix 1).

The Act established a new further education sector which is funded through the council, and to begin with is largely made up of further education and sixth form colleges previously maintained by local education authorities. The extent of the statutory duties placed upon the new bodies will be considered later in this book. The first situation which ought to be considered from a practical point of view is where a student is leaving school and intending to transfer to a local college to continue education at the age of 16 or over.

TRANSFERRING FROM SCHOOL TO COLLEGE: STUDENTS WITH STATEMENTS AND SEVERE LEARNING DIFFICULTIES

Where a young person is statemented, the provisions of the 1993 Education Act and in particular the provisions of the Disabled Persons (Services Consultation and Representation) Act 1986 mean that more rights apply to him or her. Section 5 (see Appendix 6) relates to assessment or transfer to further and higher education for statemented young persons. In practice, there are many clearly disabled persons who in fact are not statemented for one reason or another. It is not infrequent to find children with severe learning difficulties at special schools with no statement whatsoever, although it is not disputed by all those dealing with the child's problems that he or she has severe difficulties and is getting considerable expert help at school. It is also the case that some children with severe specific learning difficulties do not now have statements in certain parts of the country, where the local education authority has a number of schools within their maintained sector which provide a very large specialist amount of educational provision. In some areas, therefore, children with severe specific learning difficulties may quite justifiably not be statemented, although like other young persons with special needs, they may well require and be getting considerable help.

For practical reasons, these young persons fall into the same category as statemented children for the purposes of the preparation of their cases, but are not subject to the statutory obligation of assessment under the 1986 Act.

Where it is acknowledged that a child has severe or severe and complex learning difficulties, a statement will normally have been made. The school, whether it is an ordinary school or a specialist school, must contribute to annual reviews. The school itself, or the local education authority, will check carefully on the young person's progress, and on the young person's present condition. The required help will vary according to age, improvement or deterioration, and changing needs. A statement must be reviewed annually. The 1993 Act provides for very careful review procedures, thus extending the duty under the 1981 Act (see Appendix 3).

Save for those fortunate cases where it is apparent that the young person will not need very much, if any, individual support once transferred from school, in essence, the new act creates statutory duties which are very similar to, and possibly clearer than, those of the 1981 Education Act and its statutory replacement, the 1993 Education Act, but no real means of statutory assessment or an appeal. However, those clear duties apply to a limited class of student who requires help outside the FEFC sector. It is less clear on the general duty. There is in fact no provision similar to the 1981 and 1993 Act assessment system, just the duty to make provision. The Code of Practice (see Appendix 3) and the relevant parts of the Disabled Persons (Services Consultation and Representation) Act 1986 go a long way to fill this gap, however, particularly the Code of Practice.

In his launch Letter of Guidance of 17 July 1992, the Secretary of State asked the Further Education Funding Councils to promote cooperation between the various agencies, such as the Careers Service, Health Authorities, Social Services Department, and voluntary organisations, which are involved in providing advice or support for students with learning difficulties. The Secretary of State in his circular 1/93 similarly promotes such inter-agency corporation to ensure the best possible response to the student's needs (see Appendix 2).

Sections 5 and 6 of the Disabled Person's (Services Consultation and Representation) Act 1986 was amended by the 1992 Act. Section 5 of this act is entitled 'Disabled persons leaving special education'. Section 5(2) applies where the local education authority makes any statement in respect of a child after he or she has attained the age of 14, or if the LEA has asked an appropriate officer to give the Authority an opinion as to whether the child was disabled prior to that age, following the application of the conditions set out in Section 5(1), and the officer has answered in the affirmative. Assuming the case is governed by Section 5(2) and the answer is in the affirmative – namely, that they are disabled students – the LEA is required to pass on information about the students to the Social Services Department as they reach the end of the age of compulsory schooling, together with details of their plans for continuing education beyond that age. A young person can choose not to request help or be assessed, but if they need help in further or higher education, such an assessment should always be requested. The LEA must request help at the first review after the fourteenth birthday. It must seek information from Social Services, if it is agreed the child is disabled between twelve and eighteen months before the expected school leaving date (see Appendix 5).

In addition, LEAs are responsible for notifying the Social Services Department of the leaving dates of disabled students who will be under 19 when they leave full-time education in school, or where the authorities are responsible for them for the purposes of the 1981 Act or the 1993 Act. This includes those attending a grant-maintained school. The authority must give the appropriate officer written notification of the date when the disabled student ceases to be of compulsory school age, and of whether or not he intends to remain in full-time education and, if so, where. In the case of a disabled student over compulsory school age who is receiving full-time education either at a school or in a further or higher education institution other than a school, if he is under 19 years and 8 months the authority shall give written notice to the appropriate officer of the person's identity, his address and leaving date not less than 8 months and not more than 12 months before the leaving date.

If the authority does not know the date, but only learns of the date of leaving later on, because they were not fully aware of the person's intentions, then they shall give notice as soon as reasonably practical. Section 5(4) and Section 6 of the 1986 Act require local education authorities, for the purpose of Section 5, to keep under review the dates when the young persons are expected to cease to remain in one of their schools or in a school where they arrange provision.

THE LEA'S DUTY TO PROVIDE TRANSPORT FOR YOUNG PERSONS

The statutory duties with regard to transport remain effectively unchanged and will be considered in detail later. It continues to be a matter for LEAs to consider any arrangements necessary for the provision of transport from home to college for students with learning difficulties as for other students. This includes transport for students with learning difficulties who are attending colleges in the new further education sector, and students who are placed by the Funding Council in institutions outside the further and higher education sector where specialist provision is required. Essentially, then, this duty remains unchanged from that owed to those at school.

CONCLUSION

These are the main duties which apply, but they do not replace the assessment provision of the 1981 and 1993 Acts and their regulations, which require a very careful assessment in the process of assessing and compiling a statement. It is also to be noted that no right exists to go to an independent appeal tribunal to appeal against any decision. This issue is dealt with in more detail later. It is of considerable importance in considering preparations for the future for the young adult to realise there is no appeal. Judicial review, complaint to the Minister or complaint to the Parliamentary Commissioner or to the Local Government Commissioner are the only remedies, the first two being the only really effective methods. The third is of use only after the event complained of, as complaints to the Local Government Commission involve no power to make any compulsory order.

The 1986 Act is principally constructed to facilitate social services planning for young persons with special education needs who are assessed as being disabled. In essence, this requires local education authorities to seek a determination or assessment as to whether or not a child is a disabled person. This is dealt with in the Act by notification to the appropriate officer, who will then arrange for the social services department to carry out an assessment of that person's needs. The concept of such an assessment is not the same statutory concept of a careful assessment of a statemented child provided for under the 1981 and 1993 Acts. It does, however, provide some guidance. The actual assessment is not governed by detailed regulations and a careful statutory structure. The FEFC has, however, agreed a system which attempts to plug this gap.

It is unfortunate that the assessment and notification requirements on leaving the LEA's jurisdiction apply solely to statemented children. This does give some statutory protection, but it is very loose in comparison to that given under the 1993 Education Act to the young adult. However, apart from ensuring that the appropriate officer is notified by the local education authority, and a determination is made, whether a young person is disabled for the purposes of the 1986 Act; a statement is not necessarily a guide as to whether they require continued special educational provision. A disabled person is defined (see Section 16 of the 1986 Act) as a person to whom Section 29 of the 1948 National Assistance Act applies, i.e. 'persons who are blind, deaf or dumb, who suffer from mental disorder of any description, and other persons who are substantially and permanently handicapped by illness, injury or congenital deformity or such other disabilities as may be prescribed by the Minister'. No regulations have been made by the Minister.

This definition which includes the words, 'substantially and permanently handicapped by illness, injury of congenital deformity', is wide enough to cover all disabilities for which statements of special educational needs are made. In practice there will be normally no dispute. Dyslexia – perhaps the most controversial handicap – plainly falls into the definition of a substantial handicap as the result of illness, injury or congenital deformity. In some cases this classification will not assist a student, and a severe dyslexic, for example, may not see a benefit in these rights. It is difficult at present in practice to find any overall view as to how these provisions are in fact working. It is to be hoped that the Code of Practice under the 1993 Act improves the whole procedure.

For parents of young persons who are convinced that what is offered locally is not adequate, or where the parent is of the view that the young person would benefit from some form of residential specialist provision outside the local area despite there being some provision available locally, or simply where a parent of a young person believes that their needs are best dealt with in a different way than that which is normally available, or when a young person or their parents do not know what provision there is, it is wise to proceed as if one were preparing a case for a statement of special educational needs, on the basis that no statement has been made, but using what material is available very carefully. Even if provision seems to be adequate, a careful investigation before a place is accepted is advisable.

Chapter 2

How to Prepare the Case

Normally a young person of about average ability or better will either be leaving school at 16, or at 18 or 19: this could be following either GCSEs, A-Levels, AS-Levels, or BTech or one of the other alternatives. In general, all the young person is likely to do, and what is needed for the future ought to be the subject of consideration by the school approximately two years in advance. The parent is well advised to start preparation for the future particularly where medical and/or other reports are required two years ahead. The Code of Practice adopts this approach (see Appendix 3).

It is important, if this can be achieved, for there to be agreement between the school, and the young person and parents regarding the child's future requirements for help. If there is an agreement between the young person, the parents and the school regarding these requirements for help, then the school can do a great deal of work to assist the parent by providing educational advice to the parent in writing as to what should happen, contacting the LEA, and working with educational psychologists.

The Further and Higher Education Funding Council has published two circulars on the system for young persons with special educational needs transferring to further education. Those circulars are 93/05, and currently, 94/03, published on 28th February 1994. As both circulars have been changed slightly in 12 months, I am not proposing a detailed analysis to cover the possibility that further changes may be made and additional amended circulars issued.

The practical contents of the circulars are of some importance. Parents of young persons with special needs, or the young persons themselves, must obtain a copy of the circular. Copies can be obtained from the local FEFC Offices.

The basic system set up to cover transfer to further education is that the LEA will usually liaise with the relevant further education college as to the young person's needs, and the LEA ceases to maintain the statement once the young person has moved into further education. In these circumstances, the parents, the LEA and the young person will all have the same view as to the future, and the college will have adequate provision available for the young person.

However, where the parents and the LEA have a divergent view as to whether the child should be educated post-16, it is usual procedure for the LEA to review the young person's needs and, consequent to that review, it will amend or cease to maintain a statement. This is a decision that is subject to appeal under the Education Act 1993, and is dealt with in *Children with Special Needs, third edition*.

If a statement is to be amended, as a matter of law the LEA will be arranging the provision, and the parents deal with the LEA. It is theoretically possible, and may well happen, that exceptionally the LEA will maintain a statement, where further education colleges are involved. However, normally where a further education college is involved, the LEA will decide to cease to maintain a statement.

Where it is agreed that the young person requires a further education placement, and there is a difference of opinion between the LEA and the child's parents as to the specialist provision required, the following procedure applies. This will also apply where the LEA has successfully decided to cease to maintain a statement, and the young person is therefore in the FE sector, although unwillingly. In these circumstances, the LEA in question should generally either:

1. Send to the FEFC a recommendation setting out the parents' wishes but making it clear that the LEA itself does not support the application; or

2. Explain matters to the parents and advise them to apply directly to the FEFC.

This present procedure is covered by paragraph 11 of Annex C to the Circular 94/03.

In circumstances where the LEA does not support the parents' views, particularly in circumstances where there is not statement but a definite requirement for special educational provision, the parents may lose nothing, and probably would gain a great deal by applying themselves direct to the FEFC, having prepared their case, having discovered that the LEA does not support them. They would be better off to proceed to present their case. Obviously, the FEFC will contact the LEA, but a properly drafted application is better than a grudging approach by an LEA. However, in this situation parents, or the young person, would be well advised to be very careful as to how they prepare the application and the evidence with which they support it. In certain circumstances the FEFC will itself be prepared to commission an independent assessment to ascertain the young person's needs.

A further situation that factually has arisen causing problems with applications of this nature is in cases where young persons have been excluded from school and require specialist provision. They then become over 16 and the LEA no longer has responsibility for their case. In these cases they will cease to attend or be registered at a school, and the correct course is to apply to the FEFC under Section 4. The LEA in such circumstances is unlikely in the extreme to have made any application or reference to the FEFC, or indeed even decided what the future provision should be for the young person. In such cases, an application should be made direct to the FEFC, explaining that the LEA simply has formed no view whatsoever, due to the expulsion, and unfortunately, in many cases of this nature, the LEA sometimes not only forms no view, but is content not to provide any extra educational provision or education at all.

Having therefore considered the varying factors, I now consider what is the basic approach to the problem. In cases where the LEA makes no recommendation and in the last situation described above, the correct approach is set out below.

The Basic Approach

I approach this book on the assumption, however, that the parent or the young person is organising matters, because throughout the country the performance of local education authorities and social services departments varies considerably. The right approach to a transfer at 16 or later should be as follows:

1. Ask the questions:

    (a) What is the future plan?

    (b) Is there agreement on the young person's future? In some cases it may be clear as to what the right course of action is when the young person leaves school.

2. If the position is not clear, the young person or his parents (in the cases of more severe disablement it will normally be the parents), need to prepare the case in the following manner:

(a) Decide on what is to be the next step and if possible discuss that with the school.

(b) If the next step is a radical departure, extra help is needed for speech therapy with additional funding to pay for it, or provision outside the local area, and therefore likely to be more expensive, the parents would be well advised, if they can afford it, to obtain the advice of an independent educational psychologist at this point. If the case involves medical issues, the opinions of doctors or therapists should be obtained. This should be done well in advance.

(c) Assemble the case for the future.

(d) Finally, talk to the school, involve the LEA, and if it is wanted and obtainable, ensure an assessment is commenced under the 1986 Act.

As the 1992 Act neither creates an appeal system, nor has a formal educational assessment system – the equivalent of the statementing system – it is crucial that the case be properly organised. In cases of statemented children where there are disputes and discussions over their future, there are now a number of possible avenues which protect a child or young person. It is therefore possible to bring in new evidence, new opinions and a new approach to a case, and reprepare it so long as the case is caught in time, namely before the young person leaves school. If the young person has left school or is in a wrong or inappropriate provision, they can apply to the council by way of a direct application, without LEA support.

However, the Further and Higher Education Act only involves decisions of administrators working in the field of further and higher education for the statutory body. There is no independent appeal. It is the *preparation* of the case to be presented to those making the decision (whether a committee or individual official) that is crucial.

Chapter 3

Annual Reviews and Their Importance Under the 1992 Education Act

In cases of young persons with a statement, the nature of the annual review introduced by the 1981 Education Act is radically expanded, reformed and changed. Annual reviews are governed by the provision of Regulations 15 to 17 inclusive, of the Education (Special Educational Needs) Regulations 1994, Statutory Instrument No 1047. The conduct of annual reviews is considered in *Children with Special Needs, third edition*. Regulation 16 applies to statements for young people aged 14 where they attend school, and Regulation 17 applies to the reviews of a statement where a young person does not attend school. These are the important regulations governing the conduct of annual reviews of young persons.

The Code of Practice, made under Section 157 devotes a whole chapter (Chapter 6) to annual reviews, the relevant parts of which are in Appendix 3 to this work.

By Section 167, annual reviews must be carried out on an annual basis. The regulations provide for the system. The purpose of all annual reviews is to integrate a variety of perspectives on the child or young person's progress, to ensure that he or she is achieving the desired progress and, if necessary, to amend the statement to reflect newly identified needs and provisions. The object of the annual review at 14 is to produce a transition plan, which will draw together information from a range of individuals within and beyond the school, in order to plan carefully and accurately for the young person's transition into further education and into adult life.

The involvement of social services in the first annual review after the young person's fourteenth birthday is required under Sections 5 and 6 of the 1986 Disabled Persons Act, and the Code of Practice itself, to which local education authorities must have regard under Section 167 of the 1993 Education Act. They are required then to consult the careers service, the child health services, and any other professionals such as educational psychologists, speech therapists or occupational therapists, other psychologists, or doctors who may have a useful contribution to make.

The basic procedure is that the LEA initiates the review in writing to require the head teacher of the school to submit a review report by the specified date. The LEA must give at least two months' notice of the date by which the report is required. As with normal annual reviews, a review report is prepared; the head teacher acts as co-ordinator and must seek written advice from people specified by the LEA. The head teacher must be informed by the LEA whom he or she should invite to contribute to the review and attend the meeting. Those invited must include the child's parents, or, if the child is accommodated by the local authority, his or her carer. A relevant teacher, which may be the school's special educational needs (SEN) co-ordinator, but the choice rests with the head teacher. Where appropriate the head teacher may tell the representatives of the district health authority or social services department or other professionals closely involved that they are invited to contribute to the review summary and attend the meeting.

The head teacher has the power to invite such representatives and professionals as he or she sees fit, even if not asked to do so by the LEA. The Code of Practice suggests in such cases that the head teacher should indicate the priority attached to their attendance. Where a young person is placed outside the are of the LEA responsible for a statement, a representative of the responsible LEA and of relevant professionals such as educational psychologists should wherever possible attend the meeting.

In preparing for the review meeting, the head teacher must request written reports from the child's teachers, parents and all relevant professionals. He then summarises the evidence received and circulates a copy of that review summary to all those hoping to attend the meeting at least two weeks before the date of the meeting. Additional comments should be invited.

In annual reviews at the age of 14, the LEA must ensure that other providers such as social services are aware of the annual review and the procedures to be followed. They should always invite social services to attend, so that nay parallel assessment or work under the Disabled Persons Act 1986, the NHS and Community Care Act 1990, the Chronically Sick and Disabled Persons Act, or where power are still being exercised under the Children Act, will benefit from the information that can be drawn from the review process.

The LEA must invite the regional committee of the FEFC to be represented at the review meeting, to ensure that any information which may be required by the FEFC in determining admission arrangements to a local college or to an independent college outside the sector is collected during the review procedures. Also, The young person and his or her family must be fully informed about the full range of options.

It is particularly important that the LEA invite, as they are required to do, the careers service to be represented at the review meeting, to enable all options for careers and vocational training to be given serious consideration. The careers service will also be able to identify any specific targets which should be set as part of the annual review to ensure that independent training, personal or social skills or aspects of a wider curriculum are fully addressed in the young person's last years at school. The Code of Practice states that the plan should address the following questions:

1. What are the young person's curriculum needs during transition?

2. How can the curriculum help him or her to place his or her role in the community, and make use of leisure and recreational facilities, assume new roles in the family, develop new educational and vocational skills?

3. How can professionals develop close working relationships with colleagues and other agencies to ensure effective and coherent plans for the young person in transition?

4. Which new professionals need to be involved in planning for transition (eg. occupational therapists, careers service, other therapists)?

5. Does the young person have any special health or welfare needs which require planning and support from health and social services, now or in the future?

6. Are the assessment arrangements for transition clear, relevant and shared between all the agencies concerned?

7. How can information best be transferred from the children to adult services to ensure a smooth transition?

8. Does the young person require particular technological aids? The arrangements for a transition should include

appropriate training and arrangements for securing technological support.

9. What do the parents expect of their son or daughter?

10. What can the family contribute in terms of helping their child to develop personal and social skills, an adult lifestyle, and the acquisition of new skills?

11. Will the parents experience new care needs and require practical help in terms of aids, adaptations or general support during these years?

12. What information does the young person need in order to make informed choices?

13. What local arrangements exist to provide advocacy and advice or other relevant support services?

14. How can young persons be encouraged to contribute to their own plans and make positive decisions about the future?

15. If the young person is away from home, or attending a residential school outside their area, are there special issues relating to their return when they leave school, which require specific planning?

The transition plan which should come from the 14 years review is thereafter to be built upon. The next annual review, and later annual reviews should focus on all the aspects of the young person. Social services departments, health authorities and the careers service should be invited to be actively involved.

In such reviews, issues as to whether the powers under the Chronically Sick and Disabled Persons Act, help in the home and with adaptations in the home, should be actively considered, and raised with social services. Obviously, the same applies for those who are to be in community care, and who will require either considerable and constant attendance at home, or placement outside of the home. It is at this point where consideration must be given carefully as to whether individual care plans may be needed.

On the educational front, it is important for matters to be brought to the attention of the FEFC. In those cases where some form of provision at a specialist institution outside the sector is considered (the arrangements published in Circular 94/03 apply). But special consideration ought to be given to extra provision in a local college where an outside place is not sought or considered. For example, many young persons may be adequately catered for by their local college or a local college within reasonable travelling distance but require occupational therapy, physiotherapy and speech therapy. The health service may only be prepared or able to provide a limited amount of support, particularly with speech therapy. The FEFC has powers to arrange for extra help in this regard. These issues should be planned well in advance. The object, therefore, of the annual review is to raise all these issues, to produce a proper plan, and to ensure that the young person is not dumped in a college having left school without proper support. In cases where a child has not attended a school, due to illness or disability or some other cause, Regulation 17 adapts the annual review procedures to bear in mind that, as the young person does not attend school, it is the LEA who in this case will have full responsibility for preparing the annual review and ensuring that the plan is drafted. The Regulation is effectively the same as for that applying to young persons in schools, save for the fact that where they are not at school, the LEA takes responsibility.

The Assessment and the Contents of the Reports to be Disclosed to the Funding Council by Parents and Young Persons

Reports obviously must define the following:

1. The nature of the learning difficulty, clearly and in sufficient detail for it to be understood. The initial main report will normally be made by a psychologist. The psychologist should state bluntly where further medical evidence is needed, whether advice is needed from the speech therapy services, consultants or from other experts. If so, these reports should be obtained.

2. The level and type of support required. This may be of course capable of definition solely by an educational psychologist's report possibly read in conjunction or association with the school's views, if they agree.

3. The type of course or programme which would be suitable, together with a specification of all other necessary help. If residential provision is required this should be considered.

4. Consideration of the local placements. This will be necessary if it is to be contended that the young person requires out-of-area provision, particularly provision of a specialist nature. This will obviously require some expert input by the psychologist when looking at the local area provision, if the issue is in doubt or if it is arguable that there is something that will suit locally. The same principle applies where extra resources are requested locally, although an extension of a local provision needs to be raised with the FEFC and the college proposed.

Never submit or disclose an adverse report. If the report is a school's or is provided by social services, then they will supply it. If inaccurate or wrong it should be challenged.

Difficulties in Assessment

Experience with the 1981 Act, and the local education authorities seeking to apply it, shows that the most common complaint of parents is of delays. Where a young person is due to leave school either at 16 or later up to the age of 19, the 1993 Education Act provides for time limits. These do not apply to further and higher education transfers and assessments under the 1986 Disabled Persons Act. They do however apply to annual reviews before the young person leaves school (see Regulations 16 and 17, Appendix 4). The duty to review can therefore be enforced. It is highly likely that the most common problem in future will be delays in assessing the future requirements for provision for the young person. If there is a delay, the only remedy at the moment is judicial review or complaint to the Minister. The difficulty with a complaint to the Minister is that it would probably take too long. Judicial review in cases of young persons with disabilities is normally treated by the courts as requiring expedition and urgency, and appears at the moment to be probably the most efficient means of enforcing a rapid assessment, so that an assessment will take place in time to have relevance for the young person leaving a school or institution. Judicial review would apply to the duty to review the statement and to the 1986 Act assessment.

Indeed, in dealing with the 1992 Act, judicial reviews are effectively the only remedy for adverse decisions anyway, unless it is possible to reprepare the case and to persuade the funding council to change its mind. Persuading such a body to change its mind is obviously a difficult task. It should be borne in mind that the powers of the courts on judicial review considered later in this book are limited and do not cover factual disputes.

Although the approach of this book is to obtain, if possible, the agreement of all those advising who have had experience of, and responsibility for, the young person at school, cases will obviously arise where there is a dispute. The fact that agreement cannot be reached should not be regarded by the parents of the young person concerned as meaning that they cannot succeed in persuading the funding council to agree with their point of view. Firstly, where the young person has a view, their views are important and may often be more important than those of professionals who are in disagreement. Secondly, there may be a genuine dispute, which is why an independent educational psychologist's report, where necessary supported by medical advice, is regarded by the author as very important indeed, whether there is a disagreement or not. In all cases where there is any disagreement about any issue, other than those issues which are of minor importance, it is advisable that a meeting should be arranged between the relevant officer or officers of the funding council, to try and explain the young person's point of view, including their view of the future.

The policy of the FEFC as set out in the first two issued circulars recognises that the LEA and the young person may not agree. The policy provides for a proper consideration of a young person's case. In this area, as there are no set statutory procedures, one must rely on common sense, and proper preparation.

In making an application, parents who intend to make the application, or young persons who intend to make the application themselves should bear in mind that the local college is a separate corporate entity under the 1992 Education Act and it is to the FEFC and not to the college that application is made for provision under Section 4 of the 1992 Act. The duty under Section 4 applies to students up to the age of 25, and therefore the procedure described above in relation to annual reviews and the transition plan is equally important for those young persons who stay on at school up to the age of 18 or 19 years. The Council was asked by the Secretary of State, in his circular 92/08, to ensure that wherever possible, learning difficulties should be no bar to access to further education.

The Secretary of State also emphasised in the Circular the importance of assessing a student's educational needs and of inter-agency corporation in contributing to the arrangements that would meet those needs. The FEFC agreed criteria for taking decisions regarding funding for individual students based on the recommendations of local authorities in the context of its legal duties. These criteria are presently set out in Annex B of Circular 94/03. The arrangements set out in the Circular from the FEFC reflect the respective roles and responsibilities of the FEFC and LEAs. A formal agreement was reached between the Council and the local authority associations which recognise the important contribution made by local authorities, particularly to:

1. Assessing the educational needs of young persons with learning difficulties and/or disabilities.

2. Supporting their effective transition to further education where it is appropriate.

The function of the agreement which is Annex C to the present Circular 94/03 is to obtain a thorough assessment of the student's educational needs so that the FEFC can take appropriate decisions about a student who may require further educational provision at a specialist college outside the sector. The agreement made between the Council and the Association of County Councils and the Association of The Metropolitan Authorities covers students who wish to attend a specialist college outside the sector and they cover the following:

1. Students for whom the LEA currently has a responsibility.

2. Students for whom local sector provision is not adequate.

3. Students who come within the scope of the FEFC's legal duties.

The agreement is aimed to inform the Council about a student's needs and give a thorough assessment as an important way of helping the student identify his or her preference for appropriate further education and learning programme.

The system is that local authorities are asked to inform the FEFC about each student who comes within the scope of the agreement and for whom a place at a specialist college is considered appropriate. The LEA is asked to:

1. Make available to the Council advice on the educational needs to the individual student and supporting assessments carried out by the LEA in meeting its statutory duties under the Education Acts.

2. To identify in the context of that advice, an assessment where possible as to what extent the required provision and support is unavailable at a FEFC sector college.

3. To recommend to the Council in the context of that consideration a placement which will meet the student's needs and education outside the sector.

In considering the recommendation the local authority will take into account the student's own views which will normally be available under their most recent annual review. It will also include the student's views set out in the transition plan made on the 14 year review.

The agreement is limited in scope to the following:

1. Students rising to 16, or otherwise approaching the end of their schooling; recommendations are to be received from their home LEA.

2. For older students and/or those who have had a break from education; recommendations to be received from their home LEA if possible. In other cases it might come from another agency within the authority (e.g. social services). The Council might reasonably seek advice or information from the LEA and/or commission an independent assessment of the student's educational needs in such cases.

3. Students already attending specialist colleges outside the sector and currently supported by an LEA; recommendations to be received from their home LEA.

4. Students already attending specialist colleges outside ;the sector and originally placed by the FEFC. The Council will reasonably seek to find the views of the student's local authority and social services department and/or the careers service. The LEA might also be able to confirm historic information of provide professional expertise if this is specifically invited.

The agreement therefore is not comprehensive. It is designed mainly to deal with statemented pupils, but it accepts that the FEFC will deal with non-statemented pupils, and may need to make arrangements for their placement outside the sector. Equally, some pupils will have left the school and this may be for many reasons. However, the Circular seems to consider it an exceptional case in which a student has not had a statement. As already pointed out in this work, if the LEA in some areas has available detailed specialist provision which does not require a statement, which is quite possible, it does not follow that this is exceptional. In addition, some children with special needs are missed by the system and become young persons with special needs. In such cases the Council states that it will need a thorough assessment to be made in order to take a soundly based decision in respect of that individual student. In these circumstances a Council may be prepared to commission additional information to supplement any information available from a local authority.

As set out earlier in this chapter, if the case for the young person is properly prepared, where there is either a dispute, or no statement, or disputed recommendations, those cases in which no FEFC assessment is needed, may not be as exceptional as the FEFC consider. These cases will require much more attention to the evidence by the FEFC and the commissioning of further reports or the acceptance of reports placed before them by the parents or the young person. Cases of difficulty or dispute are cases in which it is advisable to obtain the independent advice and reports, as already suggested.

The Circular deals in particular with Section 4 of the Act, but it does not consider the additional power under Section 3 (read together with Section 4(2)) to make provision available at a local college, for example extra speech therapy. This will be much cheaper than paying for a place at a residential post-16 provision with extra speech therapy and more in keeping with the family's wishes in many cases. However, Section 4 is largely concerned with provision out of area, at a specialist institution or college. It is to be noted that the FEFC reasonably requires the student to have visited the college or institution and the college or institution to have formed the view that they can help the young person in question.

A DECISION BY THE FEFC

The Council will inform the student, his or her parent or advocate, the local authority and the recommended specialist college of the outcome of its consideration. Where the Council does not agree to secure the recommended provision, reference will be made in its decision to the FEFC's relevant criteria. Obviously, there is a legitimate expectation that the application will be considered by the published criteria issued by the FEFC, and a failure to do so would render it liable to judicial review for failing to adhere to its own procedures and thereby acting unfairly. The present criteria and factors for consideration are set out in Annex B of the Circular.

Not every published factor in Circular 94/03 is in fact determinative of an application. Without listing all 15, the fact, for example, that the educational needs have not been adequately assessed or that the parent and the young person have not been involved in the opinion of the FEFC in the process would not be fatal to any such application , so long as the application is based on an accurate assessment of the needs, is genuinely a required provision, and there are no other adequate facilities available. The criteria, therefore, published by the FEFC, include some criteria which really concerned attempting to make LEAs produce a proper assessment.

So far as a time limit is concerned, the published timetable states that the FEFC would normally expect to reach a decision within six weeks or 30 working days of a recommendation. Therefore receipt at the beginning of May should result in a determination by the middle of June. If additional information of discussion is required, more time will normally be taken.

However, on the issue of time, it should be noted that in cases where LEAs are not making a recommendation nor are likely to do so, parents and young persons would be will advised to submit the application to the FEFC very far in advance of this timetable. The timetable is designed to deal with the easy case of a recommendation by the LEA, but has no real application to cases where the LEA is not going to make a recommendation or there is a dispute as between the LEA's recommendation and the parents' and young person's views.

In such cases, as already considered in this chapter, parents and the young person should seriously consider trying to arrange a meeting, to explain their views to the FEFC, if the relevant regional office and its officials are prepared to arrange such a meeting. This will have the effect of clarifying their case.

Chapter 4

The Nature of the Duty Under the 1992 Act

GENERAL DUTIES AND POWERS OF THE FURTHER EDUCATION FUNDING COUNCIL

Section 1 of the 1992 Act establishes new Further Education Funding Councils, one for England and one for Wales. Regional Advisory Committees have also been set up under the Act. Section 2 places a duty on each funding council to secure the provision of sufficient facilities for full-time education suitable to the requirements of all 16- to 18-year-olds in their area for such education. This duty replaces the former duty of the local education authority. It must be discharged in such a way that the facilities are provided at such places, are of such character and so equipped as to be sufficient to meet the reasonable needs of all persons to whom the duty extends. This is a general target duty, the equivalent to Section 8 of the Education Act 1944, imposed upon local education authorities. The council must take account of the different abilities and aptitudes of young people, and must make effective use of resources and avoid disproportionate expenditure. It must also take into account any education provided by schools, including special schools and colleges.

Section 3 places a duty on the funding council to provide adequate facilities for part-time education for persons of any age who are over compulsory school age 16, and full-time education for those who attain the age of 19 years. This duty however only applies where the education falls into certain categories which are set out in Schedule 2 of the Act. The following courses, in summary, are included in schedule:

1. certain vocational qualifications and qualifications such as GCSEs and A-Levels.

2. basic literacy

3. basic principles of numeracy

4. access to courses of various kinds

5. English for students where English is not the language spoken at home

6. courses to teach independent living and communication skills to persons who have learning difficulties, which prepare them for entry to another course included in one of the above categories.

This is perhaps described as all courses which generally teach basic literacy, numeracy or lead to obtaining formal qualifications such as GCSEs or higher qualifications, or to professional vocational work skills courses.

The local education authority retains responsibility for non-Schedule-2 education, but this form of education is likely to be very much less important to students with learning difficulties. This is particularly as it seems largely to cover educational courses for those who wish to extend their knowledge, either on a practical or learning basis. They are not of the sort that are going to be probably of great importance to young persons with learning difficulties: the sort of matter one has in mind is practical car mechanics and practical spoken courses in languages for those who wish to go on holiday, and so forth. or use a language for work.

The LEAs' functions in respect of youth service are not affected by amendments to Section 1 of the 1944 Act which are made by the 1992 Act. They still have a duty to provide adequate facilities which includes the youth service. Section 53 of the 1944 Act imposes a duty on LEAs to secure adequate facilities for recreation, social and physical training. On the recreational side they therefore retain this important function, which obviously goes together with their functions under community care. Educationally, LEA provision is not likely to be important outside the social and recreational context.

THE ESSENTIAL DUTIES FOR YOUNG PEOPLE WITH LEARNING DIFFICULTIES

It is necessary to read Sections 3 and 4 of the 1992 Further and Higher Education Act together. Section 3 reads as follows:

3. – (1) It shall be the duty of each council to secure the provision for the population of their area of adequate facilities for education to which this subsection applies, that is –

    (a) part-time education suitable to the requirements of persons of any age over compulsory school age, and   *Part-time education, and full-time education over 18.*

    (b) full-time education suitable to the requirements of persons who have attained the age of nineteen years,

where the education is provided by means of a course of a description mentioned in Schedule 2 to this Act.

(2) A council shall discharge that duty so as –

    (a) to secure that facilities are provided at such places, are of such character and are so equipped as to meet the reasonable need for education to which subsection (1) above applies, and

(b) to take account of the different abilities and aptitudes of persons among that population.

(3) A council may secure the provision of facilities for education to which subsection (1) above applies where they are not under a duty to do so.

(4) A council shall discharge their functions under this section so as to make the most effective use of their resources and, in particular, to avoid provision which might give rise to disproportionate expenditure.

(5) In discharging those functions a council shall have regard to any education to which subsection (1) above applies provided by institutions outside the further education sector or higher education sector.

(6) The Secretary of State may by order amend Schedule 2 to this Act.

Section 4 is as follows:

4: – (1) In exercising their functions under sections 2 and 3 of this Act, each council shall (subject to the provisions of those sections) do so in accordance with subsections (2) to (4) below.

persons with learning difficulties

(2) Each council shall have regard to the requirements of persons having learning difficulties.

(3) A council shall, if they are satisfied in the case of any person among the population of their area who has a learning difficulty and is over compulsory school age but has not attained the age of twenty-five years, that –

(a) the facilities available in institutions within the further education sector or the higher education sector are not adequate for him, and

(b) it is in his best interests to do so,

secure provision for him at an institution outside those sectors.

(4) A council shall, if they are satisfied that they cannot secure such provision for a person as they are required to secure under subsection (3) above unless they also secure the provision of boarding accommodation for him, secure the provision of boarding accommodation for him.

(5) In exercising their functions under sections 2 and 3 of this Act in the case of any person who has a learning

difficulty and is over compulsory school age, a council may –

> (a) if they are satisfied that the facilities available in institutions within the further education sector or the higher education sector are not adequate for him, secure provision for him at an institution outside those sectors, and
>
> (b) secure the provision of boarding accommodation for him.

(6) subject to subsection (7) below, for the purposes of this section a person has a 'learning difficulty' if –

> (a) he has a significantly greater difficulty in learning than the majority of persons of his age, or
>
> (b) he has a disability which either prevents or hinders him from making use of facilities of a kind generally provided by institutions within the further education sector for persons of his age.

(7) a person is not to be taken as having a learning difficulty solely because the language (or form of the language) in which he is, or will be, taught is different from a language (or form of a language) which has at any time been spoken in his home.

For young persons with learning difficulties the Further and Higher Education Funding Council's duties are as follows:

1. They are required to have regard to the requirements of persons with learning difficulties.

2. Section 4(3) means that the duty extends from the ages of 16 to 25.

3. A person is defined as having a learning difficulty under Section 4(6):

   (a) if he has significantly greater difficulty in learning than the majority of persons of his age

(b) if he has a disability which either prevents or hinders him from making use of the facilities of the kind generally provided by institutions within the further education sector for persons of his age

(c) *not* solely because the language or form of language in which he is being or will be taught is different from a language or form of language which at any time is being spoken at home.

The definition of learning difficulty, therefore, is exactly the same as that under the 1981 Act and continued for children with special educational needs under the 1993 Education Act, Section 15. This is a very wide definition indeed; it basically covers all forms of disability including mild ones. The extent of this definition has been considered under the 1981 Act in *R. v. Hampshire Education Authority* ex parte *J* 84 LGR at pg. 547 Taylor J where Mr Justice Taylor made it quite clear that this is a very wide and extensive definition, covering effectively all possible learning difficulties.

The extent of the duty in Section 4 is therefore extremely wide and is owed to all those who would have fallen within the 1981 or 1993 Acts, whether or not they have statements of special educational needs. The definition in Section 1 of the 1981 Act and in the 1993 Act covers all children with learning difficulties, not just children who are the subject of a statement. See *R. v. Hampshire* supra and *R. v. The Secretary of State for Education and Science* ex parte *L* (1988) 86 LGR pg. 13.

Although, therefore, all young persons with special needs are covered by this definition, it will also apply to the case of young persons who due to disease, or who have been disabled as a result of accidents, fall within this definition. The fact, therefore, that a young person has later developed a problem, does not exclude them from this definition.

The council under Section 4(2) shall have regard to requirements of persons who have learning difficulties. In discharging their duties under Section 3 they must discharge their duties so as to:

1. secure that the facilities provided at such places are of such character and so equipped as to meet the reasonable needs of education to which subsection (1) applies

2. take account of the different abilities and aptitudes of persons among their population.

This is the general duty. Equally they have a discretion to secure these facilities where they are not under a duty to do so by Section 3(3). However, the duty considered above can be best described as a target duty equivalent to Section 8 of the 1944 Act, which gives no individual rights save the right to be educated in judicial review proceedings for young persons to secure the education which would normally be given (see *E v. Dorset County Council and Others* 1994 3 W.L.R. p.853 where Sir Thomas Bingham and Evans LJ considered the extent of the right of an individual to enforce the duty to educate).

However, Section 4, whilst lacking a mechanism such as the assessment procedure given by statute by the 1981 and 1993 Education Acts, does impose a more stringent obligation. This is imposed in Section 4(3). A council shall, if they are satisfied that in the case of any person among the population of their area who has a learning difficulty and is under 25, that (a) the facilities available in institutions within the further education sector or the higher education sector are not adequate for him, and (b) that if it in his best interest to do so, secure provision for him at an institution outside those sectors. This obligation applies to a more restricted class of persons, but not just to previously statemented pupils.

By Section 4(4), therefore, they are obliged, if they are satisfied that they cannot secure provision under Section 4(3) unless they arrange boarding accommodation for him, to secure boarding accommodation for the young person.

By Section 4(5) the council exercising functions under Sections 2 and 3 in the case of any person who has a learning difficulty who is over compulsory school age may, if they are satisfied that the facilities available in institutions within the further and higher education sector or the higher education sector are not adequate for him,

1. secure provision for him at an institution outside the sectors

2. secure the provision of boarding accommodation for him.

There is therefore a power and a duty – what, then, does Section 4(3) actually mean? The reasoning is as follows:

1. The council must be satisfied that the facilities available in institutions within the further or higher education sector are not adequate for the young person.

2. If it is in his best interests to do so then the council must secure provision including boarding accommodation, if necessary, outside that sector. This, therefore, is a mandatory duty on the basis that the council is satisfied local facilities are not adequate and the council must act in the best interests of the young person. The council must then secure provision outside its area.

This of course stresses the considerable importance of a proper assessment, and presenting a properly prepared detailed case to the council on behalf of the young person.

Section 4(5) provides that the 'council may…' and is therefore a discretionary power. It extends to the provision of boarding accommodation as well, if necessary. However, the conditions of the exercise of the discretion match Section 3(a); namely, that they must be satisfied that the facilities are inadequate. The only material difference, therefore, between Subsections (3) and (5) amounts to the fact that the 3(b) test of whether it is in the 'best interest' of the young person does not apply. In either case the council must be factually satisfied of the inadequacy of the facilities. This second discretionary power will have a practical effect where it is not necessarily 'in the best interests' of the young person. This power is very relevant where there are two sides, one arguing that he be best kept at home, and the other saying that he would be better off receiving fuller support amounting to proper provision. If the council is faced with reasonable arguments of this nature, then obviously the provisions of Section 4(5) apply. In practice, this would effectively be the difference between the two statutory provisions. The view of the young person in such a situation would, if capable of expression, be the most relevant factor.

However, for young persons with learning difficulties, these powers are important. If the FEFC does not have provision for certain types of problems, then they cannot be satisfied as a matter of law that they have adequate facilities within the relevant sector. The existence of Section 4 therefore requires a funding council to provide adequate facilities. If it does not, the effect is that it will have to pay for it elsewhere. It is to be hoped that DFE Circular 1/93 is applied. It states that adequate facilities will be provided within the local area in as many cases as possible. However, obviously the council would find it cheaper, where specialised provision is needed or for rarer forms of problems, to pay for adequate provision, as do local education authorities.

Section 4 does not require as a part of statutory policy, unlike the 1981 and 1993 Acts, education in the ordinary institution. The overall effect is to require adequate provision to be paid for, if it is not available. This obviously will apply even if it is something that ought to be available but is not available due to failure of administration and planning.

RELEVANCE OF STATEMENTS TO YOUNG PERSONS WITHOUT STATEMENTS AS APPLIED TO STATUTORY DUTY

It is important to realise that the duty under Section 4 is not restricted to young persons with statements of special educational needs. Although, therefore, the assessment procedure under the 1986 Act applies to most but not all young persons with a statement, and the annual review provisions apply under the 1993 and 1981 Acts to all statemented children, the duty to make specialised provision under the 1992 Act is not restricted to young persons with statements.

Even after the long period of time since the implementation of the 1981 Education Act, through a form of omission, many children with severe special educational needs have not been the subject of a statement. Equally, children or young persons with special educational needs can be given considerable help and not be the subject of a statement of special educational needs. However, on a practical basis, a statement of special educational needs, together with an assessment under the 1986 Act, or the use of the review procedure under the 1993 and 1981 Acts, normally with the assistance of the LEA, will be of considerable assistance where the specialist duty under Section 4 to make special educational provision either in the local area or outside the local area is relevant. The statement is not a prerequisite of any such help, neither is it a sole key to out-of-area specialist education.

Parents and young persons should not therefore decide that the case is hopeless if a young person does have a specialised need which *has* been provided for in school. In such cases, the assistance of the school should be of considerable importance, and young persons and parents should be well aware of the fact that if a request is to be made for provision, particularly under Sections 4(3) or 4(5) that they will need supporting expert reports, which can be obtained privately or under legal aid on the green form, if needed.

Although a statement will be practically a useful passport and an advantage to implementing the provisions particularly of Sections 4(3) and 4(5), it is neither essential nor is it mandatory. Where there is not a statement of special educational needs in force, the young person and his or her parents should prepare the case on exactly the same basis as those cases in which statements are current, but they will be unable to implement the 1986 Act procedures for assessment or use the annual review process. In practice, the long-term effect of the legislation may well be to include virtually all children with special educational needs who will require continuing specialist provision or who have such a prospect in the category of statemented children. However, the Code of Practice under the 1993 Act is clearly attempting to ensure that more specialist provision is given in ordinary schools to children and young persons with special educational needs, which may reduce the number of statements.

If this comes to pass, then moving pupils without statements may require such help from the FEFC, under section 4. it is likely that any such gradual reform will take time.

Chapter 5

Remedies and Judicial Review

The Act produces no statutory appeal system, and the failure of the 1993 Education Act to extend the appellate system set up under that Act to the 1992 further and higher education duties for young persons with special needs is an unfortunate omission. The Act obviously expects the parents, or the local authority working in conjunction with social services using the 1986 Act, to achieve a proper assessment. As the 1986 Act is not intended to replace the education assessment provisions of the 1981 Act, and focuses on the idea of taking care of the whole of the disabled person, particularly by the intended use of appointed representative under the Act, it is very doubtful whether the assessment procedure will in fact work as intended throughout England and Wales. Experience of the 1981 Act most unfortunately indicates that this is likely to be so. I would be pleased to report otherwise as matters develop.

Where there is delay in assessment, the only effective remedy at present is judicial review. As the young person will not have normally any means, and if under 18 would be entitled to legal aid under the Children Act. Legal aid is generally and readily available to enforce a failure to carry out statutory duties under the 1986 Act and those duties which apply to the LEA of notification and consultation. It is also available further to compel the final annual review under the 1933 Act to be timeously and properly conducted. Additionally, there is a legitimate expectation that Local Education Authorities will act fairly, and implement the procedures set out in Circular 1/93 and any further circulars which appear. There is also duty to ensure adequate consultation in the assessment of a young person with special needs and to ensure that it takes place within a reasonable time before his or her transfer. The doctrine of legitimate expectation plainly includes the expectation that local education authorities will act fairly and properly in such a process and with due expedition (see *Council of Service Unions* v. *Minister for Civil Service* (1985) 1 AC pg. 374).

REFUSAL BY THE COUNCIL

If the young person or their parents acting on their behalf is refused either a type of education available in the area, or specific form of provision which obviously would possibly include access to and provision of work processors or similar aids, or if he or she is refused a placement at an outside institution, there are effectively four remedies of which two are likely to be the most effective:

1. Complaint to the Parliamentary Commissioner about maladministration, which is only available if there is delay, maladministration or an error of law. The powers of the Commissioner are limited in any event as this is a slow process. It is not recommended where action is needed.

2. Complaint to the Minister under Sections 68 or 99 of the Education Act 1944; the Minister can only interfere if satisfied that there has been an error of law or the council is acting unreasonably.

3. Judicial review, for which legal aid is available. This is likely to be the most effective remedy.

4. If a case is badly prepared or there is new evidence then going back to the council with new evidence and persuading them that they were wrong. It depends on the facts of the case, as to whether this is realistic. If the case was properly prepared, then judicial review is appropriate, if available, but only after the care is reconsidered.

Options 3 and 4 are the realistic options where what is needed is action in cases. The Minister has fewer powers than the courts under judicial review; he is ill-equipped by comparison with a court to decide issues relating to error of law, and is likely to be much slower. On judicial review a court can only interfere if there is procedural unfairness, error of law or the authority is acting unreasonably. This means acting in a way in which no authority could reasonably act (see *Council of Civil Service Unions* v. *Minister for Civil Service* (1985) 1 AC at pg. 374). If therefore the dispute is about facts, and solely facts, then judicial review is of no use. However, many cases are likely to involve interpretations of the statutory duties, particularly under the various subsections of Section 4. If the authority has either behaved unfairly or improperly, or has arguably failed to understand the law and got it wrong, judicial review is available.

While none of these remedies is a substitute for a proper independent appeal. Legal aid is available for judicial review cases, whether under the Children Act if under 18, or under the normal legal aid provisions. Young persons are unlikely to have means if they have disabilities. A young person is therefore most likely to be eligible for legal aid.

So far as judicial review proceedings are concerned, it is important for parents and young persons to be aware that judicial review will set aside the challenged decision; it will not order the authority to grant the application save in the most exceptional circumstances. It therefore has its limitations. Full legal aid would not be available to help in the assessment procedure and in the presentation of the case to the council. Green Form legal aid is available to some for advice, however. Nonetheless, it is effectively one of the two main remedies that are likely to achieve anything, the other being old-fashioned negotiation and careful reordering of the case. For those who are consulted after a decision is made, if the case has been prepared badly or with a number of omissions, it is to be pointed out that despite the fact that it takes time, it is better to go to a court once a case is properly organised, even if a point of law is likely to be at stake and even if it requires a reapplication, than to go to court on a badly organised case, which will lose on facts.

GREEN FORM LEGAL AID AND THE ASSESSMENT PROCESS

Green Form legal aid entitles a client initially to up to what is at present £80 worth of legal advice subject to any extension. It can be possible to extend the limit so as to cover expert reports although sometimes with difficulty. However, the financial criteria are very strict as regards both income and capital. The client has to visit the solicitor in his office to sign a 'Green Form' and this is often difficult for people on income support or with disabilities. There is a procedure for someone to attend the solicitor's office to sign on the client's behalf, for which there is a special form. This procedure is potentially very important for young persons with disabilities, who are preparing a request for provision in further and higher education.

The normal financial limit is a very little indeed and will only be of use if extended to help in an assessment to obtain an expert report, or to ascertain whether the authority is in breach of its duty, entitling the claimant to Legal Aid to take the authority to court. With regards to the Green Form it is necessary to extend it by negotiation with the Legal Aid Board each time. It is however possibly that the Legal Aid Board will extend it sufficiently to cover a solicitor attending the meeting as they are prepared to cover a solicitor attending to assist a parent presenting a case under the 1981 Act process. This could also cover the 1993 Act. The Green Form scheme may cover some expenditure needed in complex cases for difficult disabilities. Nonetheless it is available.

Further expert advice is available from many charities which specialise in advising parents and young persons with disabilities, and who fall within the area of charitable support. The list of charities thought to be able to provide some help in this area, whether by way of advice, information, practical help regarding where to go, or even representation is included as an Appendix 9 to this book. Most charities provide a very important service and should most definitely not be ignored.

Chapter 6

The Remaining Relevant Duties of the LEA

The local education authority has a duty to provide adequate facilities for full-time and part-time further education of the following kinds for those in their area who are over 16: vocational, social, physical and recreational training and organised leisure time occupation (see Section 11(3) of the 1992 Act). In carrying out these functions the LEA must have regard to the requirements of persons over compulsory age who have learning difficulties. the definition of learning difficulty in Section 11(8) includes all kinds of such disabilities and mirrors the earlier definition under Section 4. This is a consistent definition continued from the 1981 Act.

In paragraph 71 of DFE Circular 3/93, the Department for Education states that the Government aim is that, so far as would be consistent with the LEAs' other obligations, learning difficulties should be no bar to access to further education.

It is a matter for LEAs to determine what facilities they should make available in pursuance of their continuing duty to ensure adequate provision of the kind not falling within Schedule 2. On discharging their duties they are required by DFE Circular 1/93 to ensure adequate arrangements exist for assessing the needs of the student with learning difficulties, and that adequate provision of such support service as is necessary is made available. The full implications of this duty, and the facilities offered under it will obviously take some time to settle down under the new system. What is of importance is that classes in a range of subjects available at adult education institutes or centres and continuing education centres for people not involved in full-time or part-time education under the Act will still be part of the LEA's statutory responsibility. These allow young adults to develop interests and skills and make new social contacts in their own community. However, the obligation plainly does not require the local education authority to offer this education to those with disabilities in a way which meets their individual needs. The duty is again a target-duty equivalent of Section 8 of the 1944 Act.

For those with more serious disabilities, of most interest will obviously be the provision of day centres or adult training centres: this will be of particular interest to the young person with a developmental disability, as this continues the work of special school in training them to take part in a life of community, and provides social training in classes in various subjects. Trainees also learn to do simple jobs. The local education authority is bound to have regard to the provision of such centres, which also meet more generally defined social needs in relation to young adults with learning difficulties.

Chapter 7

Transport to School or College

Section 55 of the Education Act 1944 requires local education authorities to make arrangements for the provision of free transport such as they consider necessary to facilitate the attendance of pupils including college students at school or college. This section has been amended by the 1992 Act to extend duties and powers of the LEA to the following:

1. For any institution in the further education sector, LEAs are required to treat full-time students at such institutions no less favourably than pupils of the same age who attend schools maintained by the LEA.

2. For students who have learning difficulties and who have been placed by the funding council in a specialist outer-sector institution, LEAs are required to treat such full-time students no less favourably than persons of the same age with learning difficulties who attend schools maintained by the LEA or any other such institution (see Schedule 8 paragraph 5).

The 1944 Act did not define the circumstances in which free transport must be provided. Section 55(3) requires the LEA to have regard to the person's age and the nature of his or her possible routes to school or college. The LEA must consider the individual circumstances of each case. In addition, the Secretary of State is empowered to make regulations requiring LEAs to publish information about their transport policy and arrangements for students aged 16 to 18, including those with learning difficulties.

In determining whether a particular person requires school transport from home to school or college, the LEA must have regard to the particular circumstances of that person (see Section 55 and *R. v. Devon County Council* ex parte *George* (1988) 3 WLR pg. 1386 House of Lords). It will not be open to an LEA to refuse provision of free transport on policy grounds, without considering the representations made to them by the young person or his or her parents as to why, in the particular circumstances of their case, policies should not be applied.

In paragraph 106 of Circular 1/93 the Secretary of State for Education sets out that he considers it reasonable for an LEA to decide that free school transport would be necessary for a post-16 pupil or student only if he or she:

1. was ordinarily resident in the area

2. attended the nearest suitable school or college, even if it was in another LEA's area or was not at school or college considered appropriate by the LEA

3. had special educational needs or learning difficulties or other individual circumstances which the LEA considered made free transport necessary.

The effect of the terms of Section 39 of the 1944 Act read together with Section 35 (see *Surrey County Council* v. *Ministry of Education* (1953) 1 WLR pg. 516, *R. v. Devon County Council ex parte George* supra) is that for secondary pupils, three miles is considered to be walking distance if there is no nearer appropriate school or college. As the amendments to Section 55 require an LEA to treat full-time students no less favourably than pupils of the same age who attend schools, if the appropriate mileage is more than three miles, obviously there is an obligation to provide transport. The provisions dealing with young persons with learning difficulties are more complex than this general rule.

For those who are treated as needing specialised provision only available in some colleges in the area but more than three miles away, or for those who are placed into a specialist institution by the funding council, then obviously the same treatment is required as for statemented pupils placed by LEAs in schools more than three miles away with special help available or at independent specialised schools or institutions. Transport should be provided. For those pupils who are so disabled as to require transport, they would normally be transported to school and there is no change in the law.

The room for argument in practical terms would appear to be where there is a college arguably within the three-mile limit which might accommodate the student, or even an LEA school. Where the Further and Higher Education Funding Council make a decision to provide particular provision in relation to a pupils at a distance, it is obviously not for the LEA to attempt to dispute the decision of the Council. If, therefore, the student does not have a choice in reality because of the decision of the Council, it is not for the LEA then to dispute the Council's decision. Where a choice is exercised by the young person where the LEA itself would not in the past provide transport, transport will not be made available, simply because a pupil is in further or higher education.

However, the discretionary power under Section 55(2) to enable LEAs to help pupils, which includes college students for whom they do not consider free school transport necessary within their travelling expenses, remains available.

In Circular 1/93 the Secretary of State requires LEAs to have clearly defined criteria by which cases are decided. The paragraph correctly concludes that there is nothing in law to say that an LEA must provide travel assistance for a person for whom they do not consider free school transport necessary, and who claims to be unable to afford the costs of his or her transport provision.

Lastly, there is Section 46 of the Public Passenger Vehicle Act 1981, which allows LEAs to use a school bus to carry those who qualify under Section 55(1) for free transport, and to carry at a charge those who do not qualify; and Section 93 of the Transport Act 1985 which allows authorities outside London to establish schemes whereby children under 17, or young people aged 17 or 18 in full-time education, can travel on public transport at concessionary rates.

Circular 1/93, paragraph 111, also states that LEAs are expected to have full regard to the possible effect of their policies on young people's willingness and ability to participate in education after the age of 16. LEAs are expected to monitor the effect of transport policies and participation rates overall, and are expected to review such policies if there is concern over this issue.

REFUSAL OF FREE OR DISCRETIONARY SCHOOL TRANSPORT

The main remedy in such a case is again judicial review. It is for the authority to exercise its discretion and decide the facts (see *R. v. Devon County Council* ex parte *George* supra). If, however, the authority has not considered parental representation or representations from the young person, has acted unfairly, or has failed to apply the correct statutory criteria, judicial review is the appropriate remedy.

Chapter 8

Other Assessments That Can Help

It was obviously the intention of parliament by amending Sections 5 and 6 of the 1986 Disabled Persons Act that the assessment procedures under the Act would operate to go on from the assessment provisions of the 1993 Education Act and the earlier 1981 Act. As already stated, this procedure lacks the clarity and effectiveness of the assessment procedures under the 1993 Education Act. There are, however, provisions for assessment under the National Health Service and Community Care Act 1990, and the Children Act 1989. There is also Section 2 of the Chronically Sick and Disabled Persons Act 1970.

Generally, under these acts, social services departments are required to assess the needs of the children and adults requiring the assistance of social services and to provide care plans to meet the individual's needs. Cooperation between social services departments, local education authorities and the funding council is very important and is stressed in all the guidance to the legislation.

THE CHILDREN ACT

The Children Act obviously applies particularly to children, which normally means young people up to the age of 18. The duties under the act are however extended by Section 24 for certain young persons who are under the age of 21. Section 24 imposes duties and confers powers upon local authorities in respect of children who are being looked after by the authority, and in respect of children and adults under 21 who were, but who are no longer, accommodated by an authority or other specific bodies. A duty is imposed upon local authorities where a child has been looked after by them to advise, assist and befriend him with a view to promoting his welfare when he ceases to be looked after under Section 23(1). This section provides for a continuing local authority responsibility to provide assistance to children and young people adjusting to leaving the environment of, for example, a community home, and adapting to independent living.

Section 24(2) defines a person qualifying for advice and assistance as:

A person within the area of the authority who is under 21 and who was at any time after reaching the age of 16 but while still a child (i.e. under 16)

(a) looked after by a local authority

(b) accommodated by or on behalf of a voluntary organisation

(c) accommodated in a Registered Children's Home

(d) accommodated:

i. by any health authority or Local Education Authority

ii. in any residential care home, nursing home or mental nursing home, for a consecutive period of at least 3 months

(e) privately fostered but who is no longer so looked after, accommodated or fostered.

In the cases of (c) to (e) above, the local authority is not required but empowered to provide advice and assistance if:

1. it appears that the person needs advice and to be befriended

2. the person asked the authority for help of a kind which they can give to those who qualify for advice and assistance.

Assistance may include making a grant to enable the person who qualifies to meet the expenses connected with his education or training, or contributing to expenses incurred by him in living near the place where he is or will be employed, is seeking employment or receiving educational training (Section 24(8)). Sections 24(6) and (7) provide the authority with power to provide assistance by cash in exceptional circumstances.

The Children Act therefore considerably extends responsibility of local authorities to children and young persons between the ages of 16 and 21 with physical or mental handicaps. It can help both in assessment of need and in provision of services to meet those needs.

ADDITIONAL DUTIES IN RELATION TO THE PROVISION OF SERVICES TO CHILDREN, YOUNG ADULTS AND FAMILIES WHICH MAY ASSIST

Part III of the Children Act gives local authorities a new range of duties, including the identification of children who are in need and provision of a range, and the level of services appropriate to those needs to enable them to fulfil a general duty to safeguard and promote the welfare of such children. Section 17(5) provides that every local authority shall facilitate the provision by others (including in particular voluntary organisations) of services which the authority has power to provide by virtue of this Section or Sections 18, 20, 23 and 24.

Section 17(10) defines a child in need as follows:

1. He is unlikely to achieve or maintain, or to have the opportunity of achieving or maintaining, a reasonable standard of help or development without the provision for him of services by a local authority under this part.

2. His health or development is likely to be significantly impaired or further impaired without the provision for him of such services or see he is disabled. Section 17(11) explains that for the purposes of this part a child is disabled if he is blind, deaf or dumb and suffers from a mental disorder of any kind or is substantially and permanently handicapped by illness, injury or cognitional deformity or other such disability such as may be prescribed.

'Development' in the Act means physical, intellectual, emotional, social or behavioural development and 'health' means physical or mental health. The child's needs will include physical, emotional and educational needs according to age, sex, race, religion, culture, language and the capacity of the current care to meet those needs.

Specific needs and duties are also provided for in Part I of Schedule 2 to the Children Act 1989. Paragraph 3 of Schedule 2 of the Act provides that the local authority may assess a child's needs for the purposes of this Act at the same time as any assessment under:

1. the Chronically Sick and Disabled Persons Act 1970

2. the Education Act 1981

3. the Disabled Persons (Services, Consultation and Representation) Act 1986

4. any other enactment providing for the recognition of the needs and complexity of multiple handicaps.

Once needs are identified, a plan needs to be developed to match service provision to the extent of the needs. This is a significant change of emphasis within the Children Act. It recognises the importance for packages of services appropriate to assess needs being planned in consultation with individual children and their families.

Local authorities are expected to act as facilitators of provision under Sections 18 (Day Care) and 20 and 23 (Accommodation) and 24 (Advice and Assistance to certain young persons aged under 21) by others as well as themselves. They must publicise the availability of such services and take account of services provided by the voluntary sector and other agencies, particularly those of particular relevance to young people such as Social Security benefits, housing or education.

The definition of a disabled child in Section 17(11) of the Act is that a child is disabled if he is blind, deaf or dumb or suffers from mental disorder of any kind or is substantially deformed or has any other such disability as may be described. The definition covers children affected by physical disability, chronic sickness, mental disability, sensory disability, communication impairment and mental illness. The Act places clear duties on local authorities to provide services for children with disabilities within their area. These services should help in the identification, diagnosis, assessment and treatment of children with physical or mental handicaps, or who are suffering from mental disorder. The local authority must cooperate with the relevant agencies, the family and the child or young person himself in assessing overall developmental needs and considering what sort of services are appropriate (see Schedule 2, Paragraph 6).

Local authorities have a duty under Section 19 and under Schedule 2, paragraph 1(12) to publish details of services available to those who might benefit. This supplements the existing lesser duty under Section 1 of the Chronically Sick and Disabled Persons Act 1970 to inform on request of relevant services provided by the authority and voluntary organisation. Section 9 of the Disabled Persons (Services, Consultation and Representation) Act 1986 amends Section 1 of the Chronically Sick and Disabled Persons Act 1970 by inserting Subsection 2(b) and extending the true scope of information a local authority is required to provide to '…any service [which is] relevant and of which particulars are in the authority's possession'.

. The publicity material should be sensitive to ethnic minorities with regard to their linguistic and cultural needs, and sensory disabilities, and should increase awareness of available services provided by the local authority and, where appropriate, by others.

Schedule 2 Paragraph 2 provides for a continuing requirement placed on local authorities to keep registers of children with disabilities in their area. Schedule 2 Paragraph 3 of the Act allows local authorities to arrange for the assessment of any child with a disability to be combined with an assessment under the Chronically Sick and Disabled Persons Act 1970, the Education Act 1981 and now 1993, the Disabled Persons (Services, Consultation and Representation) Act 1986 or any other enactment. In addition Section 27 of the Children Act states:

'(1.)Where it appears to a local authority that any authority mentioned in Subsection 3 could, by taking any specific action, help in the exercise of any of their functions under this part, they may request help of the other authority, specifying the action and questions.

(2.) An authority whose help is so requested shall comply with the request if it is compatible with its own statutory or other duties and obligations and does not unduly prejudice the discharge of any of their functions.

(3.) The other authorities are –

(a) any local authority;

(b) any local education authority;

(c) any local housing authority;

(d) any health authority; and

(e) any person authorised by the Secretary of State for the purposes of this section.'

Section 20(1) is a general provision giving power to provide accommodation for children in need within the area of the local authority, where there is no person who has parental responsibility for them or some relevantly for young adults in Section 20(1)(c); if the person who has been caring for him is unable to provide him with suitable accommodation or care. This is particularly relevant for those in case of coming out of prison.

COMMUNITY CARE SERVICES

Care services may be classified in a number of ways; these services may be specifically for the benefit of the disabled person. In this present work, to try and consider the rights of young persons with special needs in relation to community care, would be to cover many issues outside education. The National Health Service Community Care Act 1990 made detailed amendments to the powers of local authorities to provide local community care. The main object was to implement the recommendation of the Griffiths Report in 1988 that social services authorities should have the task of ensuring that the needs of individuals within specified groups are identified, plans of care devised, and services coordinated.

Firstly, each local authority social services department will have to prepare and publish a strategic plan for the provision of community services in their area which must be reviewed and up dated from time to time (see Section 46).

Community care services are those provided under Part 3 of the 1948 National Assistance Act, including Sections 21 and 29, Section 45 of the Health Service and Public Health Act 1968, Section 21 and Schedule 8 of the National Health Service Act 1977 and Section 117 of the Mental Health Act 1983 (see Section 46(3) of the 1990 Act).

A plan should assess the needs in the locality, including the need to rehabilitate patients, and set out strategies for meeting the needs. The plan should develop a mixed economy of care making use of voluntary private providers, wherever this is most cost-effective.

The authority is responsible for assessing individual needs for these services. It has a duty to carry out an assessment in accordance with the directions given by the Secretary of State where it has the power to provide a range of services for a person who may be in need of them (Section 47). The district health authority and the local housing authority should be brought into the assessment when necessary (Section 47(3)). Having made the assessment, the authority must then decide whether the person's needs call for the needs services provided at public expense. It might be possible to make some charge, depending on the type of service and what the client can afford.

So far as their relevance to education is concerned, the community care provisions obviously have relevance for young persons who have mental or physical disabilities, or both. Again, the provisions of the Act effectively now give two routes to enforce the duly. Firstly, there is the possibility for complaint to the Minister under the complaint provisions of the National Health Service Act. This has plain limitations, as do complaints to the Department for Education considered before in this work. Secondly, there is judicial review. In cases of delay, error of law, unfairness or breach of statutory duty, judicial review is the most effective remedy. Legal Aid is available on the basis considered before, however, it is also of relevance to note that the Department for Education probably has much greater expertise than other ministries in dealing with complaints and appellate problems because of the history of the 1981 Education Act in the appeal powers. In the case of these particular duties, therefore, there is all the more reason to consider the issue of judicial review.

Further and Higher Education Act 1992

CHAPTER I RESPONSIBILITY FOR FURTHER EDUCATION

The new funding councils

1. The Further Education Funding Councils

The new further education sector

2. Full-time education for 16 to 18 year-olds
3. Part-time education, and full-time education for those over 18
4. Persons with learning difficulties

Finance

5. Administration of funds by councils
11. Functions of local education authorities in respect of further education

1. The Further Education Funding Councils (1) There shall be established–

(a) a body corporate to be known as the Further Education Funding Council for England to exercise in relation to England the functions conferred on them, and

(b) a body corporate to be known as the Further Education Funding Council for Wales to exercise in relation to Wales the functions conferred on them.

(2) The Further Education Funding Council for England shall consist of not less than twelve nor more than fifteen members appointed by the Secretary of State, of whom one shall be so appointed as chairman.

(3) The Further Education Funding Council for Wales shall consist of not less than eight nor more than twelve members appointed by the Secretary of State, of whom one shall be so appointed as chairman.

(4) In appointing the members of a council the Secretary of State–

(a) shall have regard to the desirability of including persons who appear to him to have experience of, and to have shown capacity in, the provision of education or to have held, and to have shown capacity in, any position carrying responsibility for the provision of education and, in appointing such persons, he shall have regard to the desirability of their being currently engaged in the provision of further education or in carrying responsibility for such provision, and

(b) shall have regard to the desirability of including persons who appear to him to have experience of, and to have shown capacity in, industrial, commercial or financial matters or the practice of any profession.

(5)   In this Part of this Act any reference to a council is to a further education funding council.

(6)   References in the Education Acts to the appropriate further education funding council, in relation to any educational institution–

(a) where the institution mainly serves the population of England, are to the Further Education Funding Council for England and, where the institution mainly serves the population of Wales, are to the Further Education Funding Council for Wales, and

(b) where the institution receives financial support from a further education funding council, are to that council also (if different).

(7)   Any dispute as to whether any functions are exercisable by one of the councils shall be determined by the Secretary of State.

(8)   Schedule 1 to this Act has effect with respect to each of the councils.

THE NEW FURTHER EDUCATION SECTOR

2. Full-time education for 16 to 18 year-olds (1) It shall be the duty of each council to secure the provision for the population of their area of sufficient facilities for education to which this subsection applies, that is, full-time education suitable to the requirements of persons over compulsory school age who have not attained the age of nineteen years.

(2)   That duty extends to all persons among that population who may want such education and have not attained the age of nineteen years.

(3)   A council shall discharge that duty so as–

(a) to secure that the facilities are provided at such places, are of such character and are so equipped as to be sufficient to meet the reasonable needs of all persons to whom the duty extends, and

(b) to take account of the different abilities and aptitudes of such persons.

(4)   A council may secure the provision of facilities for education to which subsection (1) above applies for persons to whom that duty does not extend.

(5)   A council shall discharge their functions under this section so as to make the most effective use of the council's resources and, in particular, to avoid provision which might give rise to disproportionate expenditure.

(6)   In discharging those functions a council shall have regard to any education to which subsection (1) above applies provided by schools maintained by local education authorities, grant-maintained schools, special schools not maintained by local education authorities, city technology colleges or city colleges for the technology of the arts.

3. Part-time education, and full-time education for those over 18 (1) It shall be the duty of each council to secure the provision for the population of their area of adequate facilities for education to which this subsection applies, that is–

(a) part-time education suitable to the requirements of persons of any age over compulsory school age, and

(b) full-time education suitable to the requirements of persons who have attained the age of nineteen years,

where the education is provided by means of a course of a description mentioned in Schedule 2 to this Act.

(2)   A council shall discharge that duty so as–

(a) to secure that facilities are provided at such places, are of such character and are so equipped as to meet the reasonable need for education to which subsection (1) above applies, and

(b) to take account of the different abilities and aptitudes of persons among that population.

(3)   A council may secure the provision of facilities for education to which subsection (1) above applies where they are not under a duty to do so.

(4)   A council shall discharge their functions under this section so as to make the most effective use of their resources and, in particular, to avoid provision which might give rise to disproportionate expenditure.

(5)   In discharging those functions a council shall have regard to any education to which subsection (1) above applies provided by institutions outside the further education sector or higher education sector.

(6)   The Secretary of State may by order amend Schedule 2 to this Act.

4 Persons with learning difficulties (1) In exercising their functions under sections 2 and 3 of this Act, each council shall (subject to the provisions of those sections) do so in accordance with subsections (2) to (4) below.

(2)   Each council shall have regard to the requirements of persons having learning difficulties.

(3)   A council shall, if they are satisfied in the case of any person among the population of their area who has a learning difficulty and is over compulsory school age but has not attained the age of twenty-five years, that–

(a) the facilities available in institutions within the further education sector or the higher education sector are not adequate for him, and

(b) it is in his best interests to do so,

secure provision for him at an institution outside those sectors.

(4)   A council shall, if they are satisfied that they cannot secure such provision for a person as they are required to secure under subsection (3) above unless they also secure the provision of boarding accommodation for him, secure the provision of boarding accommodation for him.

(5)   In exercising their functions under sections 2 and 3 of this Act in the case of any person who has a learning difficulty and is over compulsory school age, a council may–

(a) if they are satisfied that the facilities available in institutions within the further education sector or the higher education sector are not adequate for him, secure provision for him at an institution outside those sectors, and

(b) secure the provision of boarding accommodation for him.

(6)   Subject to subsection (7) below, for the purposes of this section a person has a 'learning difficulty' if–

(a) he has a significantly greater difficulty in learning than the majority of persons of his age, or

(b) he has a disability which either prevents or hinders him from making use of facilities of a kind generally provided by institutions within the further education sector for persons of his age.

(7)   A person is not to be taken as having a learning difficulty solely because the language (or form of the language) in which he is, or will be, taught is different from a language (or form of a language) which has at any time been spoken in his home.

FINANCE

5.   Administration of funds by councils (1) A council may give financial support to the governing body of any institution within the further education sector or the higher education sector in respect of–

(a) the provision of facilities for further education, or

(b) the provision of facilities, and the carrying on of any activities, which the governing body of the institution consider necessary or desirable to be provided or carried on for the purpose of or in connection with the provision of facilities for further education.

(2)   A council may give financial support to the governing body of any institution within the further education sector in respect of–

(a) the provision of facilities for higher education, or

(b) the provision of facilities, and the carrying on of any activities, which the governing body of the institution consider necessary or desirable to be provided or carried on for the purpose of or in connection with the provision of facilities for higher education.

(3)   A council may give financial support to a further education corporation for the purposes of any educational institution to be conducted by the corporation, including the establishment of such an institution.

(4)   For the purposes of section 4(3) to (5) of this Act, a council may give financial support to any person other than a local education authority, the governing body of a grant-maintained school or a person maintaining or carrying on a city technology college or city college for the technology of the arts.

(5)   A council may give financial support to any person in respect of–

(a) the provision of training or advice, or

(b) the carrying on of research or other activities,

relevant to the provision of facilities for further education.

(6)   Financial support under this section–

(a) shall take the form of grants, loans or other payments, and

(b) may be given on such terms and conditions as the council think fit.

(7)   The terms and conditions on which a council make any grants, loans or other payments under this section may in particular–

(a) enable the council to require the repayment, in whole or in part, of sums paid by the council if any of the terms and conditions subject to which the sums were paid is not complied with, and

(b) require the payment of interest in respect of any period during which a sum due to the council in accordance with any of the terms and conditions remains unpaid,

but shall not relate to the application by the person to whom the financial support is given of any sums derived otherwise than from the council.

(8)   A council may not give any financial support except in accordance with this section.

Functions of Local Education Authorities in Respect of Further Education

11.   For section 41 of the Education Act 1944 (functions of local education authorities in respect of further education) there is substituted–

'Functions of local education authorities in respect of further education:
41.–(1) It shall be the duty of every local education authority to secure the provision for their area of adequate facilities for further education.

(2)   Subsection (1) above does not apply to education to which section 2(1) or 3(1) of the Further and Higher Education Act 1992 applies, but in respect of education to which section 3(1) of that Act applies a local education authority may–

(a) secure the provision for their area of such facilities as appear to them to be appropriate for meeting the needs of the population of their area; and

(b) do anything which appears to them to be necessary or expedient for the purposes of or in connection with such provision.

(3)   Subject to subsection (4) below and section 14(1) to (4) of the Further and Higher Education Act 1992, in this Act 'further education' means–

(a) full-time and part-time education suitable to the requirements of persons over compulsory school age (including vocational, social, physical and recreational training); and

(b) organized leisure-time occupation provided in connection with the provision of such education.

(4) In this Act 'further education' does not include higher education or secondary education.

(5) In subsection (3)(b) above 'organized leisure time occupation' means leisure-time occupation, in such organized cultural training and recreative activities as are suited to their requirements, for any persons over compulsory school age who are able and willing to profit by facilities provided for that purpose.

(6) A local education authority may secure the provision of further education for persons from other areas.

(7) In exercising their functions under this section a local education authority shall have regard to any educational facilities provided by institutions within the higher education sector or the further education sector, and other bodies, which are provided for, or available for use by persons in, their area.

(8) In exercising their functions under this section a local education authority shall also have regard to the requirements of persons over compulsory school age who have learning difficulties.

(9) Subject to subsection (10) below, for the purposes of subsection (8) above a person has a 'learning difficulty' if–
   (a) he has a significantly greater difficulty in learning than the majority of persons of his age; or
   (b) he has a disability which either prevents or hinders him from making use of facilities of a kind generally provided in pursuance of the duty under subsection (1) above for persons of his age.

(10) A person is not to be taken as having a learning difficulty solely because the language (or form of the language) in which he is, or will be, taught is different from a language (or form of a language) which has at any time been spoken in his home.

(11) A local education authority may do anything which appears to them to be necessary or expedient for the purposes of or in connection with the exercise of their functions under this section.'

Courses of Further Education
Schedule 2

General This Schedule sets out the descriptions of courses referred to in section 3(1) of the Act. The Further Education Funding Councils will have a duty to secure adequate provision of these courses for part-timers aged over 16 and full-timers aged 19 and over. The duty in respect of other courses will rest with LEAs.

The descriptions of courses of further education referred to in section 3(1) of this Act are the following–

(a) a course which prepares students to obtain a vocational qualification which is, or falls within a class, for the time being approved for the purposes of this sub-paragraph by the Secretary of State,

(b) a course which prepares students to qualify for–

    (i) the General Certificate of Secondary Education, or

    (ii) the General Certificate of Education at Advanced Level or Advanced Supplementary Level (including Special Papers),

(c) a course for the time being approved for the purposes of this sub-paragraph by the Secretary of State which prepares students for entry to a course of higher education,

(d) a course which prepares students for entry to another course falling within paragraphs (a) to (c) above,

(e) a course for basic literacy in English,

(f) a course to improve the knowledge of English of those for whom English is not the language spoken at home,

(g) a course to teach the basic principles of mathematics,

(h) in relation to Wales, a course for proficiency or literacy in Welsh,

(i) a course to teach independent living and communication skills to persons having learning difficulties which prepares them for entry to another course falling within paragraphs (d) to (h) above.

DFE Circular 1/93, 5 January 1993
The Further and Higher Education Act 1992
Relevant Extracts

1. This Circular explains the main provisions of the Further and Higher Education Act 1992, with particular reference to how they will affect local education authorities (LEAs) in England.

2. Part I of the Circular describes the establishment of the new Further Education Funding Council, which will take over from LEAs with effect from 1 April 1993 statutory duties in respect of the provision of full-time education for those aged 16–18. The Council will also take over duties in respect of part-time education for those over compulsory school age and full-time education for those aged 19 and over which falls within Schedule 2 to the Act. A new further education sector will be established, funded through the Council, and made up largely of further education and sixth form colleges formerly maintained by LEAs. Arrangements are described whereby institutions which remain maintained or assisted by LEAs can apply for funding from the Council. The duty on a number of bodies, including LEAs, to provide information to the Funding Council is also described.

3. Part II of the Circular outlines the arrangements for the transfer of property, rights, liabilities and staff.

4. Part III of the Circular describes the requirements for statutory proposals affecting the education of pupils aged 16–18 in schools in consequence of the establishment of the new further education sector.

5. Part IV of the Circular describes the new framework for LEAs' duties and powers after April 1993. LEAs will continue to have power to provide sixth form education in schools. They will have a duty to secure adequate provision of those aspects of further education which do not fall to the Funding Council. These functions will be recognised in the funding arrangements for local authorities. LEAs will also have a power to secure the provision of further education where the Further Education Funding Council has the duty to secure provision. Authorities will no longer be obliged to have schemes of local management for further education, but will be able to establish governing bodies for their remaining maintained further education institutions and to delegate funds and powers to them. LEAs will have a duty to keep under review the quality and standards of education in their institutions, and a power of inspection. Recoupment for further education will become claimable only with the consent of the home authority.

6. Part V of the Circular deals with further education in schools. From August 1993, the governing bodies of maintained schools will have the power to decide to put on further education in their schools. Under certain conditions, adults and part-timers may be educated alongside school pupils.

7. Part VI of the Circular deals with implications for other functions of LEAs:
   - discretionary awards;
   - transport to colleges;
   - prison education;
   - specific grants; and
   - careers and educational guidance.

It also deals with some minor amendments to education and other legislation.

8. The Education Bill which is currently before Parliament would affect some of the provisions of the Further and Higher Education Act 1992. Guidance on the new legislation will issue, subject to its enactment.

9. The explanations given in the Circular do not constitute an authoritative legal interpretation of the legislation: that is a matter for the courts.

I The new further education sector

12. **The Further Education Funding Council** On 17 July 1992, the Secretary of State announced the appointment of members of the Further Education Funding Council for England, established under section 1 of the Further and Higher Education Act 1992.

13. With effect from 1 April 1993, the Further Education Funding Council will have the duty:
   i to secure the provision of sufficient facilities for full-time education for those over compulsory school age and under 19 (section 2); and
   ii to secure the provision of adequate facilities for part-time education for those over compulsory school age, and full-time education for those aged 19 and over, in relation to the types of education listed in Schedule 2 to the Act (section 3). Schedule 2 is reproduced as an Annex to this Circular.

In carrying out these duties the Council must have regard to the requirements of people with learning difficulties (section 4).

14. In his letter of guidance of 17 July 1992, the Secretary of State drew the Further Education Funding Council's attention to the importance of liaison with LEAs in order to fulfil its responsibilities for post-16 education and to facilitate progression between the sectors.

15. Also with effect from 1 April 1993, a new further education sector will be established which will comprise (i) institutions conducted by further education corporations and (ii) institutions designated under section 28 of the Act.

16. **Further education corporations** The new sector will consist mostly of institutions currently maintained by local education authorities which have

been incorporated as further education corporations. Those included in the initial round of incorporation were:

- further and higher education institutions which have at least 15 per cent of their students (in full-time equivalent terms) attending full-time or on release from employment; and
- sixth form colleges, other than voluntary aided sixth form colleges (which will be designated as part of the new sector under section 28).

The main Order giving the names of the colleges incorporated under section 15 of the Act came into force at the end of September and was circulated to LEAs. A small number of colleges which would have been incorporated under section 15 but for the fact that they have only recently been established will be incorporated under section 16 of the Act. A draft Order giving the names of these colleges was circulated to relevant LEAs and colleges on 26 October 1992. The Order was laid before Parliament on 2 December 1992 and is expected to come into force on 29 December.

17. Further education corporations created under section 15 were established on 30 September 1992, when they became eligible to receive financial assistance from the Council in respect of their preparations for independence. The corporations which are to be created in the initial round of incorporation under section 16 should be established by the end of December and will then become eligible to receive similar financial assistance. The corporations will take over the running of their institutions on 1 April 1993. For further education colleges, the initial members of the new corporations consist of the members of the existing college governing bodies, except for any governor who was nominated and appointed by the LEA, or any governor who is an elected member of a local authority or is employed by a local authority other than as a teacher or as a member of a fire brigade. All corporations must have a member nominated by the local Training and Enterprise Council. For sixth form colleges, where the membership needed to be brought closer to that of the further education model, the Secretary of State has appointed the initial members of the corporations which will conduct the colleges. The existing governing bodies of further education and sixth form colleges will exist in parallel with the corporations until 31 March 1993. The governing bodies will continue to be responsible for running the colleges until that time. The corporations will plan for the future and take decisions on matters relating to the colleges after 31 March 1993.

18. Section 16 provides for incorporation of further LEA maintained institutions in the following circumstances:

i.   any maintained further education institution which comes to have 15 per cent of its student load attending on a full-time or released basis (calculated in accordance with Schedule 3 to the Act);

ii. any maintained institution which becomes a tertiary or sixth form college; and

iii. under section 16(3), any maintained further education institution which does not have 15 per cent of its student load attending on a full-time or released basis, where incorporation is recommended by the Further Education Funding Council.

It is a requirement of section 51 of the Act that proposals must be published by the Secretary of State or the Council, as appropriate, before incorporation takes place under section 16. Regulations prescribing the form of the proposals, the time within which they must be published and the manner in which they must be published came into force on 28 October 1992. They also prescribe the publication arrangements where the Council proposes to recommend the dissolution of any further education corporation by the Secretary of State under section 27 of the Act. They require proposals published by the Councils for the establishment or dissolution of a further education corporation to be sent in draft form to the relevant LEA.

19. The Secretary of State has asked the Council to consider urgently any applications from institutions seeking incorporation in 1993 under section 16(3). In its circular letter of 22 October 1992, the Council set out the criteria against which it would consider any applications under section 16.

20. Designated institutions Institutions to be designated as part of the new sector under section 28 will comprise voluntary aided sixth form colleges, the Workers' Educational Association and thirteen institutions which are currently assisted by an LEA or are grant-aided by the Department for Education. These are the six long-term residential colleges for adults, four colleges funded through the London Residuary Body (City Literary Institute, Morley College, Mary Ward Centre, Working Men's College), Cordwainers College, the National Sea Training College and the College of the Sea. These institutions already have governing bodies with their own legal status. A draft order giving the names of institutions to be designated was circulated to LEAs on 28 August 1992.

64. LEA functions for further education Section 11 of the Further and Higher Education Act 1992 sets out LEAs' functions in relation to further education on and after 1 April 1993. The duty placed upon LEAs by the Education Act 1944 is changed only in its scope, not in its substance. Section 11 of the 1992 Act amends section 41 of the Education Act 1944 to exclude from LEAs' duties those now placed on the Further Education Funding Council under sections 2(1) and 3(1) of the 1992 Act. Accordingly, LEAs' duty is to secure the provision for their area of adequate facilities for courses not falling within Schedule 2. In so doing they must take account of facilities already provided by other bodies, such as further or higher education institutions or voluntary bodies. LEAs retain a power to finance the provision of Schedule 2 courses where they decide to do so.

65. The definition of further education is altered from that introduced by the Education Reform Act 1988 only in respect of clarifying the boundary with secondary education. Under section 14, full-time education suitable to the requirements of 16 to 18 year olds is defined as further education, except where provided in schools when it is defined as secondary education.

66. LEAs' functions in respect of the Youth Service are not affected by the amendments to section 41 of the 1944 Act. The further education for which they have a duty to provide adequate facilities includes the Youth Service. The definition of further education includes vocational, social, physical and recreational training, as well as organised leisure-time occupation provided in association with such activities. The provision of the Youth Service for those of school age is covered by Section 53 of the 1944 Act which imposes a duty on LEAs to secure adequate facilities for recreation and social and physical training.

67. During the passage of the Further and Higher Education Bill, the then Secretary of State gave an assurance that, in calculating the transfer of funds from local authorities to the new sector, the Government would leave within local authority standard spending the resources attributable to those courses for which LEAs would remain responsible. It was made clear that the Government's further education reforms would not themselves cause fees for such courses to rise. Fees policy in respect of courses which LEAs fund, including concessionary arrangements, remains as now for each LEA to decide.

68. The transfer of responsibilities for further education has been reflected in the local authority funding settlement for 1993–94. In arriving at a figure for the amount to transfer from local authority finance, careful account was taken of the division of expenditure, assessed on the basis of a survey of LEAs' spending, between the further education courses which will remain with LEAs and those further education courses for which responsibility transfers to the Further Education Funding Council.

69. It is for LEAs to determine how to carry out their duty to secure the provision of further education. They may make use of their own maintained adult institutions, independent adult institutions, schools (including grant-maintained schools) in consultation with the governing bodies (see paragraphs 95–96), voluntary bodies such as the Workers' Educational Association, and colleges within the further education sector. It will be important to maintain and develop progression routes from courses provided in pursuit of LEAs' duties to those which fall within Schedule 2. To that end, LEAs will wish to liaise and collaborate with local colleges in the further education sector. They will need to do so particularly in relation to section 6(5) applications (see paragraphs 21–27), and to courses which colleges in the further education sector put on under contract with LEAs.

70. Grants for Education Support and Training (GEST) in support of LEA grants to the Workers' Educational Association will continue in 1993–94. The WEA is to be designated for funding by the Further Education Funding Council, which will take over the grant currently paid to the WEA by the Department. The funding for the WEA which was transferred to LEAs in 1990 will continue to be reflected in local authority funding. LEAs' duty to secure adequate further education outside the scope of Schedule 2 makes a continuing role in funding the WEA appropriate. Many LEAs are likely to find the support of WEA courses valuable in carrying out that duty. GEST funding has been successful in promoting mutually beneficial collaboration between LEAs and the WEA.

71. Students with learning difficulties LEAs' duties and powers in relation to further education (see paragraph 64) apply equally to students with learning difficulties. Moreover, in exercising those functions, LEAs continue to be under a specific duty, under section 11(8) of the Act, to have regard to the requirements of this group of students. The definition of the term learning difficulty, which is carried over from previous legislation, includes all types of disability. The Government's aim is that, so far as is consistent with LEAs' other obligations, learning difficulties should be no bar to access to further education.

72. It remains a matter for LEAs to determine what facilities they should make available in pursuit of their continuing duty to ensure that adequate provision, of the kind not falling within Schedule 2, is available for those aged 19 and over with learning difficulties. In discharging this duty, LEAs should ensure that adequate arrangements exist for assessing the needs of these students and identifying the provision that will be appropriate, and for the provision of such support services as are necessary. Where students with learning difficulties are moving from LEA provision to the new further education sector, LEAs will need to liaise in appropriate cases with colleges and the Further Education Funding Council to ensure the identification of suitable provision. Information about the individual's needs which has been built up during a period of LEA provision, and possibly incorporated in a statement, will be of particular value to the assessment. Account should, however, be taken of the views of the individual concerned about the confidentiality of this information.

73. For young people with statements who remain in school after age 16, LEAs remain under a duty to provide for them in accordance with their statements. This means, for example, that an LEA is required to fund a place for an individual in an independent special school, if his or her statement specifies that form of provision.

74. In his launch letter of guidance of 17 July 1992, the Secretary of State asked the Further Education Funding Council to promote collaboration between the various agencies, such as the careers service, health authorities, social services departments and voluntary organisations, which are involved in providing advice or support for students with learning difficulties. The Secretary of State invites LEAs similarly to promote such inter-agency co-operation to ensure the best possible response to students' needs.

75. To assist the student's transition from the LEA sector to the further education sector, the new Act amends sections 5 and 6 of the Disabled Persons (Services, Consultation and Representation) Act 1986. The new provisions require LEAs to pass information about all disabled students to the social services department as they reach the end of compulsory schooling, together with details of their plans for continuing education beyond that age. LEAs remain responsible for notifying the social services department of the leaving dates of disabled students who will be under 19 when they leave full-time education from a school where authorities are responsible for them for the purposes of the Education Act 1981; this includes a grant-maintained school.

76. As indicated in paragraphs 104–114, it continues to be a matter for LEAs to consider any arrangements necessary for the provision of transport from home to college for students with learning difficulties, as for other students. This includes transport for students with learning difficulties who are attending colleges in the new further education sector, and such students who have been placed by the Further Education Funding council in institutions outside the further and higher education sectors. The assessment arrangements under consideration by the Council involve LEAs being aware at an early stage of proposals for such placements, which will enable them to consider the need for transport to be provided in individual cases.

V Further education in schools

90. Governing bodies' powers and responsibilities Section 12 of the Further and Higher Education Act 1992 comes into force on 1 August 1993. It gives a power to the governing bodies of LEA-maintained schools to provide certain types of further education (part-time education suitable to the requirements of persons over compulsory school age or full-time education suitable to the requirements of those aged 19 and over). For the purposes of the Education Acts, people receiving further education in schools are not defined as pupils. Governing bodies of maintained schools other than special schools have the responsibility of deciding whether or not to provide such further education. In the case of special schools, the consent of the LEA is required before further education is provided or ceases to be provided.

91. Further education may be provided either conjointly with school education, or separately. There are no limits on governors' powers to provide the education separately, though they will need to consider carefully the financial implications and the market for the further education which they wish to put on. Such education might be put on in the evenings, during the holidays, or in spare classrooms during the school day.

92. Under section 12, the Secretary of State intends to make Regulations which will allow governors to determine for themselves the circumstances in which adults and pupils may be educated together in the same room, provided that there is at all times supervision by a member of the school's teaching staff. Governors will, of course, wish to exercise their discretion in such a way as to ensure that the education and well-being of their pupils are protected. Guidance to the education service on child protection (although not specifically about the education of adults and pupils together) is given in DES Circular 4/88, 'Working Together for the Protection of Children from Abuse: Procedures within the Education Service'. Regulations will be made during 1993 and come into force prior to the commencement of the 1993/94 academic year. Draft Regulations will be the subject of consultation in the spring.

93. Statutory proposals under the 1944 and 1980 Acts Since governing bodies alone will be responsible for deciding whether to provide further education in a school, section 9 of the Education Act 1944 is amended to make it clear that LEAs do not themselves have the power to establish a school specifically to provide further education as well as primary or secondary education. For the same reasons, section 13 of the Education Act 1980 is amended to provide that the Secretary of State may not approve proposals that a new or existing school should be maintained as a voluntary school by an LEA if the school is also to provide further education. A further amendment to section 13 of the 1980 Act allows voluntary schools to provide further education without being obliged to follow statutory procedures for a significant change of character. Since LEAs may not assume the power given to governors to provide further education, section 12 of the 1980 Act does not need to be similarly amended.

94. Use of schools' budgets Amendments are made to the Education Reform Act 1988 to provide that expenditure by LEAs on the provision of further education in schools must be excluded from the calculation of the authority's general schools budget; that the allocation formula under a Local Management of Schools (LMS) scheme of delegation may not take into account people receiving further education at a school; and that governors may not vire expenditure within their LMS budgets into the provision of further education courses. None of the cost of a school's provision of further education should therefore be borne on the resources provided to the school under LMS. It is of course possible for an LEA to provide the governors with separate funds to spend on further education, and they will wish to do so where the LEA carry out part of their duties in relation to further education through the school. Where education provided by the governing body falls within Schedule 2, it is open to the governing body to apply via a college within the further education sector under section 6(5) for support from the Further Education Funding Council (see paragraphs 21–27). In other cases, where there is expenditure arising from the provision of further education which is not met from elsewhere, the cost will need to be recovered from fees charged to the persons receiving the education. Governors may set their own charge and the prohibition in section 106 of the Education Reform Act 1988 on charging fees for admission to maintained schools has been disapplied in respect of such provision.

Home to school/college transport post-16

104. LEAs' transport duties and powers under section 55 of the Education Act 1944 already apply to pupils and students over compulsory school age. Section 55(1) requires LEAs to make such arrangements for the provision of free transport and otherwise as they consider necessary, or as the Secretary of State may direct, to facilitate the attendance of pupils (including college students) at schools, or at institutions they maintain or assist which provide further or higher education (or both). Section 55(2) enables LEAs to help pupils (including college students) for whom they do not consider free transport necessary with their travelling expenses.

105. Section 55 will be amended by paragraph 5 of Schedule 8 to the Further and Higher Education Act from 1 April 1993 to–

i.   a.   extend LEAs' transport duties and powers to students at any college in the further education sector; and

b.   require LEAs to treat such full-time students no less favourably than pupils of the same age who attend schools maintained by an LEA;

ii. a.   extend LEAs' transport duties and powers to students who have learning difficulties and who have been placed by the Further Education Funding Council at an institution outside the further and higher education sectors; and

b.   require LEAs to treat such full-time students no less favourably than–
(1) persons of the same age with learning difficulties who attend schools maintained by an LEA; or
(2) where there are no such arrangements, such persons whose education the LEA have arranged at any other institution.

iii. enable the Secretary of State to make Regulations requiring LEAs to publish information about their transport policy and arrangements for college students aged 16 to 18, including those with learning difficulties. The Regulations will be made during the summer and come into force by the end of June.

106. The 1944 Act does not define the circumstances which make free transport necessary, although section 55(3) requires LEAs to have regard (amongst other things) to a person's age and the nature of his or her possible routes to school or college.

107. But it is important to note that LEAs are obliged, in determining whether in the case of a particular person the provision of transport from home to school or college is necessary, to have regard to the particular circumstances of that person. Thus, it would not be open to an LEA to refuse the provision of free transport on policy grounds, without considering any representations made to them by the person or his or her parents as to why in the particular circumstances of their case that policy should not be followed.

108. In practice, the Secretary of State would probably consider it reasonable for an LEA to decide that free transport would be necessary for a post–16 pupil or student only if he or she–

i.   was ordinarily resident in their area;

ii. attended the nearest suitable school or college, even if it was in another LEA's area or was not the school or college considered appropriate by the LEA; and

iii. had special educational needs or learning difficulties or other individual circumstances which the LEA considered made free transport 'necessary'.

109. LEAs have wide powers to help those for whom they do not consider free transport necessary. Section 55(2) of the 1944 Act enables LEAs to help such persons with part or all of their travelling expenses, as the LEA think fit. If LEAs take means into account in deciding whether to provide such assistance, they should have clearly defined criteria by which such cases are decided. However, there is nothing in law to say that an LEA must provide travel assistance for a person for whom they do not consider free transport necessary, and who claims to be unable to afford the cost of his or her transport.

110. In addition, section 46 of the Public Passenger Vehicles Act 1981 allows LEAs to use a school bus carrying those who qualify under section 55(1) for free transport to carry at a charge those who do not qualify; and section 93 of the Transport Act 1985 allows authorities outside London to establish schemes whereby children under 17, or young people aged 17 or 18 in full-time education, can travel on public transport at concessionary rates.

111. The Secretary of State hopes that, in considering their use of their transport duties and powers, LEAs will have full regard to the possible effect of their policies on young people's willingness and ability to participate in education after the age of 16. He expects that LEAs will monitor the effects of transport policies on participation rates overall, and will review such policies if there is any cause for concern. The Secretary of State will himself keep this aspect of the new arrangements under review.

112. The Secretary of State also hopes that LEAs will continue to think it right to give assistance with transport or travel expenses to those who attend the nearest suitable school or college of their parents' denomination, even though a suitable non-denominational school or college might be nearer their homes.

113. The Secretary of State considers it desirable for LEAs to change their transport policies only at the beginning of an academic year, and for the changes to apply only to 16 year-olds entering school sixth forms or colleges, unless changes are required to comply with the legislation that takes effect from 1 April 1993.

114. Where LEAs wish to change their transport policy, the Secretary of State considers that fairness requires an LEA to carry out an adequate consultation. LEAs should consult pupils or students and their parents who benefit, or who might reasonably expect to benefit, from their transport policy about any proposals to withdraw or reduce the provision under that policy, before reaching a decision. The Secretary of State further hopes that LEAs will not withdraw or reduce the transport provision they make for post–16 pupils or students who have chosen or who already attend a school or college on the basis, in part, of that provision.

115. Prison education The Home Office is responsible for education for prisoners throughout HM Prison Service establishments. That responsibility is not affected by the provisions of the Further and Higher Education Act 1992. In June 1992, the Home Office indicated that it would be changing the arrangements whereby it invited LEAs to provide this service and was moving towards competitive tendering. All existing providers, including local education authorities and further education colleges, have been invited to tender. In its letter of 23 October 1992 to all LEAs, the Department for Education clarified the position regarding prison education staff. The Department's circular letter of 12 November 1992 on the transfer of staff also refers (see paragraph 50 above). The contract terms and conditions provide that, where there is a change in the provider, the successful contractor should offer interviews to existing staff.

Extract Code of Practice 1993 Education Act

ANNUAL REVIEWS

Annual Reviews from Age 14–19

6:42. Some pupils with statements of special educational needs will remain in school after the age of 16. LEAs remain responsible for such pupils until they are 19. Others with statements will, however, leave school at 16, moving, for example, to a college within the further education sector or to social services provision. But, whatever the intended future destination of the young person, the annual review has an additional significance as he or she approaches the age of 16.

6:43. The first annual review after the young person's 14th birthday should involve the agencies who will play a major role during the post-school years. The transfer of relevant information should ensure that young people receive any necessary specialist help or support during their continuing education and vocational or occupational training after leaving school. For young people with disabilities, the role of social services departments will be of particular importance and local authorities have specific duties relating to other legislation which are set out below.

The first annual review after the young person's fourteenth birthday

6:44. The annual review procedure described above applies with the following exceptions:

- the LEA convene the review meeting, even when the young person is at school. The LEA must invite the child's parents and relevant member of staff, any people specified by the head teacher, and anyone else the LEA consider appropriate
- the LEA must also ensure that other providers, such as social services, are aware of the annual review and the procedures to be followed, and must invite the social services department to attend the review so that any parallel assessments under the Disabled Persons Act (1986); the NHS and Community Care Act 1990; and the Chronically Sick and Disabled Persons Act 1970 can contribute to and draw information from the review process
- the LEA must invite the careers service to be represented at the review meeting, to enable all options for further education, careers and occupational training to be given serious consideration. The careers service will also be able to identify any specific targets which should be set as part of the annual review to ensure that independence training,

personal and social skills, and other aspects of the wider curriculum are fully addressed during the young person's last years at school

- the LEA prepare the review report and the Transition Plan after the meeting, and circulate these to the young person's parents, the head teacher, all those from whom advice was sought, all those attending the review meeting and any others the LEA consider appropriate. In particular, the LEA should consider passing the review report and Transition Plan to the FEFC, particularly in cases where a decision might need to be taken about specialist college provision outside the further education sector (see also paragraphs 6:56–6:58).

The Transition Plan

6:45. The first annual review after the young person's 14th birthday and any subsequent annual reviews until the child leaves school should include a **Transition Plan** which will draw together information from a range of individuals within and beyond the school in order to plan coherently for the young person's transition to adult life. Under sections 5 and 6 of the Disabled Persons Act 1986, at the first review after a child's 14th birthday LEAs must seek information from social services departments as to whether a child with a statement under Part III of the Education Act 1993 is disabled and may require services from the local authority when leaving school. LEAs should also consult child health services and any other professionals such as educational psychologists, therapists or occupational psychologists who may have a useful contribution to make.

6:46. The Transition Plan should address the following questions:
The School

- What are the young person's curriculum needs during transition? How can the curriculum help the young person to play his or her role in the community; make use of leisure and recreational facilities; assume new roles in the family; develop new educational and vocational skills?

The Professionals

- How can they develop close working relationships with colleagues in other agencies to ensure effective and coherent plans for the young person in transition?

- Which new professionals need to be involved in planning for transition, for example occupational psychologists; a rehabilitation medicine specialist; occupational and other therapists?

- Does the young person have any special health or welfare needs which will require planning and support from health and social services now or in the future?

- Are assessment arrangements for transition clear, relevant and shared between all agencies concerned?

- How can information best be transferred from children's to adult services to ensure a smooth transitional arrangement?

- Where a young person requires a particular technological aid, do the arrangements for transition include appropriate training and arrangements for securing technological support?
- Is education after the age of 16 appropriate, and if so, at school or at a college of further education?

The Family
- What do parents expect of their son's or daughter's adult life?
- What can they contribute in terms of helping their child develop personal and social skills, an adult life-style and acquire new skills?
- Will parents experience new care needs and require practical help in terms of aids, adaptations or general support during these years?

The Young Person
- What information do young people need in order to make informed choices?
- What local arrangements exist to provide advocacy and advice if required?
- How can young people be encouraged to contribute to their own Transition Plan and make positive decisions about the future?
- If young people are living away from home or attending a residential school outside their own LEA, are there special issues relating to the location of services when they leave school which should be discussed in planning?
- What are the young person's hopes and aspirations for the future, and how can these be met?

6:47. The Transition Plan should build on the conclusions reached and targets set at previous annual reviews, including the contributions of teachers responsible for careers education and guidance. It should focus on strengths as well as weaknesses and cover all aspects of the young person's development, allocating clear responsibility for different aspects of development to specific agencies and professionals. LEAs should advise schools on the proper balance of the transition programme components and ensure that all relevant information is available, together with advice and support as required. Social services departments, the health services and the careers service should be actively involved in the plan.

Involvement of social services departments
6:48. The first annual review after a child's 14th birthday will have a special significance because of the LEA's duties under Sections 5 and 6 of the Disabled Persons (Services, Consultation and Representation) Act 1986. Sections 5 and 6 of that Act require LEAs to seek information from social services departments as to whether a child with a statement under Part III of the Education Act 1993 is disabled and may require services from the local authority when leaving school. The LEA must inform the appropriate and designated officer of the relevant social services department of the date of the child's first annual review after his or her 14th birthday and must similarly inform the social

services department (if it is agreed that the child in question is disabled) between eight and 12 months before the expected school leaving date. LEAs may also inform social services departments at any time *after* the particular annual review required under Section 5 of the Disabled Persons Act if it is considered that circumstances have changed and the young person concerned may now be considered to be disabled.

6:49. LEAs and, so far as reasonable, schools should familiarise themselves with the following Acts, which may directly affect the future provision available to a young person with special educational needs:

The Chronically Sick and Disabled Persons Act 1970

The Employment and Training Act 1973 as amended by the Trade Union Reform and Employment Rights Act 1993

The Disabled Persons (Services, Consultation and Representation) Act 1986

The Children Act 1989

The National Health Service and Community Care Act 1990

The Further and Higher Education Act 1992

6:50. Under the Children Act 1989 and the NHS and Community Care Act 1990, social services departments are required to arrange a multi-disciplinary assessment and provide care plans for children and adults with significant special needs – which may include the provision of further education facilities.

6:51. The transition period may be associated with increasing levels of disability in some young people. It may therefore be necessary to plan for future increased special needs and for the provision of aids and adaptations both in a home and an educational setting. Young people may choose **not** to be assessed as disabled under Sections 5 and 6 of the Disabled Persons Act and may similarly choose **not** to request help through the local authority community care arrangements. The LEA should give details of any relevant voluntary organisation or professional agency providing advice and counselling if such advice is needed. Schools should have information available on local sources of help and advice, including any local disability organisations which can provide information on the wider range of local services and offer independent advice and advocacy if required.

6:52. Local authority social services departments have duties under Section 24 of the Children Act 1989 to make arrangements for young people over 18 who are regarded as being 'in need' and who have been looked after by the local authority or received services from them prior to that date. LEAs should therefore ensure that the young person is aware of the power of the social services department to provide assistance beyond the age of 18 and provide any relevant information to the social services department in question in order to alert them of any potential special needs. Where a young person has been looked after in a foster placement or a residential home or attended a residential school outside his or her own local authority, the LEA should seek to ensure liaison between all relevant LEAs and social services departments.

The role of the careers service

6:53. The careers service must be invited to the first annual review following the young person's 14th birthday; and should also be invited to all subsequent annual reviews. Vocational guidance should be presented in the wider context of information on further education and training courses and should take fully into account the wishes and feelings of the young person concerned. The careers officer with specialist responsibilities should provide continuing oversight of, and information on, the young person's choice of provision, and assist the LEA and school in securing such provision and providing advice, counselling and support as appropriate. In some circumstances careers officers may also wish to involve occupational psychologists, who can contribute to the development of a vocational profile of a young person for whom future planning is giving cause for concern. Schools may in particular welcome guidance on curriculum development in independence, social or other skills, and ways of involving young people themselves in assessment and in strategies to address any behavioural or other problems which may otherwise adversely affect their further education or future employment.

6:54. Records of Achievement should be used, with the young person's consent, to provide information to colleges or any other provision to which the young person may move on leaving school. Where appropriate, Records of Achievement can be produced in Braille as well as in print, can make use of pictorial or abstract symbol systems, and may include a range of illustrative material (including supporting photographs, tapes or videos) which provide information on the young person.

Information

6:55. Circular 93/05 (B19/93 in Wales) from the Further Education Funding Council contains advice on the Council's arrangements for funding placements for students with learning difficulties and disabilities. It is the FEFC's responsibility in such circumstances to ensure that an assessment is made when such young people enter further education; in practice the LEA conducts the assessment on the FEFC's behalf in many cases. Circular 93/05 states that the assessment should be based upon:

- the availability to young people and their advocates of a full range of information from the LEA about post-16 education and training choices, to inform placement decisions as indicated in the Parent's Charter

- the involvement of young people, their parents and their advocates in the assessment process, and

- the advice, wherever possible, of a range of professionals to ensure expert guidance, including for example careers officers, educational psychologists and other specialists who have knowledge of the individual's needs.

Transfer to the further education sector

6:56. LEAs should ensure that where a young person has a statement of special educational needs, a copy of the statement together with a copy of the most recent annual review (together with any advice or information appended to it including the Transition Plan) should be passed to the social services department and the college or other provision that the young person will be attending. Where a decision might need to be taken by the FEFC about the placement of a student in a specialist college outside the FE sector, a copy of the Transition Plan should be sent to the FEFC. LEAs should seek the agreement of students and parents to the transfer of information (including statements) from school to the further education sector, but should explain the importance of such information and the desirability of the transfer.

6:57. Where students or their families consider that the information contained in the statement or annual review presents a negative picture or is inaccurate in some way, the LEA should consider how the review process can be made more positive and participative at the time of transition so that the conclusions of the last annual review are seen as an action plan for future development. The LEA should consider including in the review report information such as Records of Achievement which present the student in a positive light and provide information about his or her wider interests and abilities. The LEA should seek the consent of parents and students prior to the final annual review for the transfer of the review report and any Records of Achievement to the FEFC.

6:58. Schools should foster links with local further education colleges. This will help in the decision-making process and in the eventual transition itself, easing the move for both young person and staff at the further education college. Link provision with colleges can be of particular benefit to a young person with special educational needs by providing opportunities for integration, extending the curriculum and offering an induction into the adult environment of further education.

The involvement of young people in assessment and review

6:59. The views of young people themselves should be sought and recorded wherever possible in any assessment, reassessment or review during the years of transition. Some young people may wish to express these views through a trusted professional, family, independent advocate or adviser, the Named Person or through an officer of the authority. Effective arrangements for transition will involve young people themselves addressing issues of:

- personal development
- self-advocacy
- the development of a positive self-image
- awareness of the implications of any long-term health problem or disability and
- the growth of personal autonomy and the acquisition of independent living skills.

6:60. If the growth of these personal skills is to complement the student's progress through agreed academic and vocational curriculum arrangements and to inform choices about continuing education and future employment, student involvement on a regular basis in the annual review process should be encouraged.

Encouraging student involvement in decision-making during transition:
- schools and LEAs should consider ways of ensuring that students' views are incorporated in planning for transition – for example the use of student counsellors, advocates or advisers, the Named Person, social workers or peer support
- curriculum planning should focus on activities which encourage students to review and reflect upon their own experiences and wishes and to formulate and articulate their views
- the student will need to come to terms with the wider implications of his or her disability or special need in adult life. Careful attention should be given to the avoidance of stigmatising language or labels and to the provision of accurate and sensitive advice and information on any aspects of the disability or special need as required
- transition should be seen as a continuum. Students should be encouraged to look to the future and plan how they will develop the academic, vocational, personal and social skills necessary to achieve their long-term objectives. Records of Achievement can demonstrate success and enable young people to recognise and value their own achievements as a contribution to their future learning and adult status and
- students will be most effectively involved in decision-making when supported by information, careers guidance, counselling, work experience and the opportunity to consider a wide range of options during the transition phase.

Students without statements but with special educational needs
6:61. In some instances, a student approaching the age of 16 may have special educational needs which do not call for a statement, but which are likely to require some support if he or she goes on to further education. To ensure that these students are able to make decisions, and to facilitate their successful transition, it is important that they have appropriate help and guidance. This might include the provision of school/college link courses or work placements and should involve the different local agencies concerned. Further education colleges will need a thorough assessment of the young person's needs in order to make soundly based decisions about appropriate provision.

6:62. Schools providing support to students through the school-based stages of assessment should therefore consult as appropriate with other relevant services, such as the careers service, to ensure that relevant, detailed information is transferred to the FEFC, with the young person's consent. The LEA should provide schools with information on transition to the FE sector and details of local and national voluntary organisations which may help such students and their families. In some cases, schools may wish to prepare their own transition plans for students with special educational needs, but without a statement.

Review of statement where child aged 14 attends school

16.–(1) This regulation applies where –

  (a) an authority review a statement under section 172(5) other than on the making of an assessment,

  (b) the child concerned attends a school, and

  (c) the review is the first review commenced after the child has attained the age of 14 years.

(2) The authority shall for the purpose of preparing a report under this regulation by notice in writing require the head teacher of the child's school to seek the advice referred to in regulation 15(4), including in all cases advice as to the matters referred to in regulation 15(4)(e), from –

  (a) the child's parent,

  (b) any person whose advice the authority consider appropriate for the purpose of arriving at a satisfactory report and whom they specify in the notice referred to above, and

  (c) any person whose advice the head teacher considers appropriate for the purpose of arriving at a satisfactory report.

(3) The authority shall invite the following persons to attend a meeting to be held on a date before the review referred to in paragraph (1) is required to be completed –

  (a) the child's parent;

  (b) a member or members of the staff of the school who teach the child or who are otherwise responsible for the provision of education for the child whose attendance the head teacher considers appropriate and whom he has asked the authority to invite;

  (c) a representative of the social services authority;

  (d) a person providing careers services under sections 8 to 10 of the Employment and Training Act 1973(i);

  (e) any person whose attendance the head teacher considers appropriate and whom he has asked the authority to invite; and

  (f) any person whose attendance the authority consider appropriate.

(4) The head teacher shall not later than two weeks before the date on which the meeting referred to in paragraph (3) is to be held serve on all the persons invited to attend that meeting copies of the advice he has received pursuant to his request under paragraph (2) and shall by written notice request the recipients to submit to him before or at the meeting written comments on that advice and any other advice which they think appropriate.

(5) A representative of the authority shall attend the meeting.

(6) The meeting shall consider the matters referred to in regulation 15(7), in all cases including the matters referred to in regulation 15(4)(e), and shall

make recommendations in accordance with regulation 15(8) and (9), in all cases including recommendations as to the matters referred to in regulation 15(8)(c).

(7) The report to be prepared by the authority under paragraph (2) shall be completed after the meeting, shall contain the authority's assessment of the matters required to be considered by the meeting and their recommendations as to the matters required to be recommended by it and shall refer to any difference between their assessment and recommendations and those of the meeting.

(8) The authority shall within one week of the date on which the meeting was held send copies of the report completed under paragraph (7) to –

(a) the child's parent;

(b) the head teacher;

(c) the persons from whom the head teacher sought advice under paragraph (2);

(d) the persons who were invited to attend the meeting under paragraph (3); and

(e) any person to whom they consider it appropriate to send a copy.

(9) The authority shall review the statement under section 172(5) in light of the report and any other information or advice which it considers relevant, shall make written recommendations as to the matters referred to in regulation 15(8)(a) and (b), and shall prepare a transition plan.

(10) The authority shall within one week of completing the review under section 172(5) send copies of the recommendations and the transition plan referred to in paragraph (9) to the persons referred to in paragraph (8).

Review of statement where child does not attend school

17.–(1) This regulation applies where an authority review a statement under section 172(5) other than on the making of an assessment and the child concerned does not attend a school.

(2) The authority shall prepare a report addressing the matters referred to in regulation 15(4), including the matters referred to in regulation 15(4)(e) in any case where the review referred to in paragraph (1) is commenced after the child has attained the age of 14 years or older, and for that purpose shall seek advice on those matters from the child's parent and any other person whose advice they consider appropriate in the case in question for the purpose of arriving at a satisfactory report.

(3) The authority shall invite the following persons to attend a meeting to be held on a date before the review referred to in paragraph (1) is required to be completed –

(a) the child's parent;

(b) where the review referred to in paragraph (1) is the first review commenced after the child has attained the age of 14 years, a representative of the social services authority;

(c) where subparagraph (b) applies, a person providing careers services under sections 8 to 10 of the Employment and Training Act 1973; and

(d) any person or persons whose attendance the authority consider appropriate.

(4) The authority shall not later than two weeks before the date on which the meeting referred to in paragraph (3) is to be held send to all the persons invited to that meeting a copy of the report which they propose to make under paragraph (2) and by written notice accompanying the copies shall request the recipients to submit to the authority written comments on the report and any other advice which they think appropriate.

(5) A representative of the authority shall attend the meeting.

(6) The meeting shall consider the matters referred to in regulation 15(7), including in any case where the review is commenced after the child has attained the age of 14 years the matters referred to in regulation 15(4)(e), and shall make recommendations in accordance with regulation 15(8) and (9), including in any case where the child has attained the age of 14 years or older as aforesaid recommendations as to the matters referred to in regulation 15(8)(c).

(7) The report prepared by the authority under paragraph (2) shall be completed after the meeting referred to in paragraph (3) is held, shall contain the authority's assessment of the matters required to be considered by the meeting and their recommendations as to the matters required to be recommended by it, and shall refer to any difference between their assessment and recommendations and those of the meeting.

(8) The authority shall within one week of the date on which the meeting referred to in paragraph (3) was held send copies of the report completed under paragraph (7) to –

(a) the child's parent;

(b) the persons from whom they sought advice under paragraph (2);

(c) the persons who were invited to attend the meeting under paragraph (3); and

(d) any person to whom they consider it appropriate to send a copy.

(9) The authority shall review the statement under section 172(5) in light of the report and any other information or advice which it considers relevant, shall make written recommendations as to the matters referred to in regulation 15(8)(a) and (b), in any case where the review is the first review commenced after the child has attained the age of 14 years prepare a transition plan, and in any case where a transition plan exists amend the plan as they consider appropriate.

(10) The authority shall within one week of completing the review under section 172(5) send copies of the recommendations and any transition plan referred to in paragraph (9) to the persons referred to in paragraph (8).

Reviews
1993 Statutory Instrument No 1047

REVIEW OF STATEMENT IN YEARS OTHER THAN THAT OF CHILD'S 14TH BIRTHDAY WHERE HE ATTENDS SCHOOL

15.–(1) This regulation applies where–

(a) an authority review a statement under section 172(5);

(b) the child concerned attends a school; and

(c) the child will not attain the age of 14 years during the academic year in which the report referred to in paragraph (2) is required to be completed.

(2) The authority shall by notice in writing require the head teacher of the child's school to submit a report to them under this regulation by a specified date not less than two months from the date the notice is given and shall send a copy of the notice to the child's parent.

(3) The head teacher shall for the purpose of preparing the report referred to in paragraph (2) seek advice as to the matters referred to in paragraph (4) from–

(a) any person whose advice the authority consider appropriate for the purpose of arriving at a satisfactory report and whom they specify in the notice referred to in paragraph (2); and

(b) any person whose advice the head teacher considers appropriate for the purpose of arriving at a satisfactory report.

(4) The advice referred to in paragraph (3) shall be written advice as to–

(a) the child's progress towards meeting the objectives specified in the statement;

(b) the child's progress towards attaining any targets established in furtherance of the objectives specified in the statement;

(c) where the school is a maintained, grant-maintained or grant-maintained special school, the application of the provisions of the National Curriculum to the child;

(d) where the school is a maintained, grant-maintained or grant-maintained special school, the application of any provisions substituted for the provisions of the National Curriculum in order to maintain a balanced and broadly based curriculum;

(e) where appropriate, and in any case where a transition plan is required to be prepared under paragraph (12), any matters which are the appropriate subject of such a plan;

(e) whether the statement continues to be appropriate;

(f) any amendments to the statement which would be appropriate; and

(g) whether the authority should cease to maintain the statement.

(5) The notice referred to in paragraph (2) shall require the head teacher to invite the following persons to attend a meeting to be held on a date before the report referred to in that paragraph is submitted–

(a) the representative of the authority specified in the notice;

(b) the child's parent;

(c) a member or members of the staff of the school who teach the child or who are otherwise responsible for the provision of education for the child whose attendance the head teacher considers appropriate;

(d) any other person whose attendance the head teacher considers appropriate; and

(e) any person whose attendance the authority consider appropriate and who is specified in the notice.

(6) The head teacher shall not later than two weeks before the date on which a meeting referred to in paragraph (5) is to be held send to all the persons invited to that meeting a written summary of the advice he has received pursuant to his request under paragraph (3) and by written notice accompanying the copies shall request the recipients to submit to him before or at the meeting written comments on the summary and any other advice which they think appropriate.

(7) The meeting referred to in paragraph (5) shall consider–

(a) the matters referred to in paragraph (4); and

(b) any significant changes in the child's circumstances since the date on which the statement was made or last reviewed.

(8) The meeting shall recommend–

(a) any steps which it concludes ought to be taken, including whether the authority should amend or cease to maintain the statement;

(b) any targets to be established in furtherance of the objectives specified in the statment which it concludes the child ought to meet during the period until the next review; and

(c) where a transition plan is required to be prepared under paragraph (12), the matters which it concludes ought to be included in that plan.

(9) If the meeting cannot agree the recommendations to be made under paragraph (8) the persons who attended the meeting shall make differing recommendations as necessary.

(10) The report to be submitted under paragraph (2) shall be completed after the meeting is held and shall include the head teacher's assessment of the matters referred to in paragraph (7) and his recommendations as to the matters referred to in paragraph (8), and shall refer to any difference between his assessment and recommendations and those of the meeting.

(11) When the head teacher submits his report to the authority under paragraph (2) he shall at the same time send copies to–

(a) the child's parent;

(b) the persons from whom the head teacher sought advice under paragraph (3);

(c) the persons who were invited to attend the meeting in accordance with paragraph (5);

(d) any other person to whom the authority consider it appropriate that a copy be sent and to whom it directs him to send a copy; and

(e) any other person to whom the head teacher considers it appropriate that a copy be sent.

(12) The authority shall review the statement under section 172(5) in light of the report and any other information or advice which they consider relevant, shall make written recommendations as to the matters referred to in paragraph (8)(a) and (b) and, where the child will attain the age of 15 years or older during the academic year in which the report referred to in paragraph (2) is required to be completed, shall prepare a transition plan.

(13) The authority shall within one week of completing the review under section 172(5) send copies of the recommendations and any transition plan referred to in paragraph (12) to–

(a) the child's parent;

(b) the head teacher;

(c) the persons from whom the head teacher sought advice under paragraph (3);

(d) the persons who were invited to attend the meeting in accordance with paragraph (5); and

(e) any other person to whom the authority consider it appropriate that a copy be sent.

REVIEW IN YEAR OF CHILD'S 14TH BIRTHDAY WHERE HE ATTENDS SCHOOL

16.–(1) This regulation applies where–

(a) an authority review a statement under section 172(5);

(b) the child concerned attends a school; and

(c) the child will attain the age of 14 years during the academic year in which the review is required to be completed.

(2) The authority shall for the purpose of preparing a report under this regulation by notice in writing require the head teacher of the child's school to seek the advice referred to in regulation 15(4), including in all cases advice as to the matters referred to in regulation 15(4)(e), from–

(a) any person whose advice the authority consider appropriate for the purpose of arriving at a satisfactory report and whom they specify in the notice referred to above; and

(b) any person whose advice the head teacher considers appropriate for the purpose of arriving at a satisfactory report.

(3) The authority shall invite the following persons to attend a meeting to be held on a date before the review referred to in paragraph (1) is required to be completed–

(a) the child's parent;

(b) a member or members of the staff of the school who teach the child or who are otherwise responsible for the provision of education for the child whose attendance the head teacher considers appropriate and whom he has asked the authority to invite;

(c) a representative of the appropriate further education funding council;

(d) a representative of the social services authority;

(e) a person providing careers services under sections 8 to 10 of the Employment and Training Act 1973(g);

(f) any person whose attendance the head teacher considers appropriate and whom he has asked the authority to invite; and

(g) any person whose attendance the authority consider appropriate.

(4) The head teacher shall not later than two weeks before the date on which the meeting referred to in paragraph (3) is to be held serve on all the persons invited to attend that meeting a copy of a written summary of the advice he has received pursuant to his request under paragraph (2) and shall by written notice request the recipients to submit to him before or at the meeting written comments on that advice and any other advice which they think appropriate.

(5) A representative of the authority shall attend the meeting.

(6) The meeting shall consider the matters referred to in regulation 15(7), in all cases including the matters referred to in regulation 15(4)(e), and shall make recommendations in accordance with regulation 15(8) and (9), in all cases including recommendations as to the matters referred to in regulation 15(8)(c).

(7) The report to be prepared by the authority under paragraph (2) shall be completed after the meeting, shall contain the authority's assessment of the matters required to be considered by the meeting and their recommendations as to the matters required to be recommended by it and shall refer to any difference between their assessment and recommendations and those of the meeting.

(8) The authority shall within one week of the date on which the meeting was held send copies of the report completed under paragraph (7) to–

(a) the child's parent;

(b) the head teacher;

(c) the persons from whom the head teacher sought advice under paragraph (2);

(d) the persons who were invited to attend the meeting under paragraph (3); and

(e) any person to whom they consider it appropriate to send a copy.

(9) The authority shall review the statement under section 172(5) in light of the report and any other information or advice which they consider relevant,

shall make written recommendations as to the matters referred to in regulation 15(8)(a) and (b), and shall prepare a transition plan.

(10) The authority shall within one week of completing the review under section 172(5) send copies of the recommendations and the transition plan referred to in paragraph (9) to the persons referred to in paragraph (8).

REVIEW OF STATEMENT WHERE CHILD DOES NOT ATTEND SCHOOL

17.–(1) This regulation applies where an authority review a statement under section 172(5) and the child concerned does not attend a school.

(2) The authority shall prepare a report addressing the matters referred to in regulation 15(4), including the matters referred to in regulation 15(4)(e) in any case where the child will attain the age of 14 years or older during the academic year in which the review referred to in paragraph (1) is required to be completed, and for that purpose shall seek advice on those matters from any person whose advice they consider appropriate in the case in question for the purpose of arriving at a satisfactory report.

(3) The authority shall invite the following persons to attend a meeting to be held on a date before the review referred to in paragraph (1) is required to be completed–

(a) the child's parent;

(b) where the child will attain the age of 14 years during the academic year in which the review referred to in paragraph (1) is required to be completed, a representative of the appropriate further education funding council;

(c) where the child will attain the age of 14 years during the academic year in which the review referred to in paragraph (1) is required to be completed, a representative of the social services authority; and

(d) any person or persons whose attendance the authority consider appropriate.

(4) The authority shall not later than two weeks before the date on which the meeting referred to in paragraph (3) is to be held send to all the persons invited to that meeting a copy of the report which they propose to make under paragraph (2) and by written notice accompanying the copies shall request the recipients to submit to the authority written comments on the report and any other advice which they think appropriate.

(5) A representative of the authority shall attend the meeting.

(6) The meeting shall consider the matters referred to in regulation 15(7), including in any case where the child will attain the age of 14 years or older during the academic year in which the review is required to be completed the matters referred to in regulation 15(4)(e), and shall make recommendations in accordance with regulation 15(8) and (9), including in any case where the child will attain the age of 14 years or older as aforesaid recommendations as to the matters referred to in regulation 15(8)(c).

(7) The report prepared by the authority under paragraph (2) shall be completed after the meeting referred to in paragraph (3) is held, shall contain

the authority's assessment of the matters required to be considered by the meeting and their recommendations as to the matters required to be recommended by it, and shall refer to any difference between their assessment and recommendations and those of the meeting.

(8) The authority shall within one week of the date on which the meeting referred to in paragraph (3) was held send copies of the report completed under paragraph (7) to–

   (a) the child's parent;

   (b) the persons from whom they sought advice under paragraph (2);

   (c) the persons who were invited to attend the meeting under paragraph (3); and

   (d) any person to whom they consider it appropriate to send a copy.

(9) The authority shall review the statement under section 172(5) in light of the report and any other information or advice which it considers relevant, shall make written recommendations as to the matters referred to in regulation 15(8)(a) and (b), and in any case where the child will attain the age of 14 years or older during the academic year in which the review is required to be completed prepare a transition plan.

(10) The authority shall within one week of completing the review under section 172(5) send copies of the recommendations and any transition plan referred to in paragraph (9) to the persons referred to in paragraph (8).

TRANSFER OF STATEMENTS

18.–(1) This regulation applies where a child in respect of whom a statement is maintained moves from the area of the authority which maintains the statement ('the old authority') into that of another ('the new authority').

(2) The old authority shall transfer the statement to the new authority, and from the date of the transfer the statement shall be treated for the purposes of the new authority's duties and functions under Part III of the Act and these Regulations as if it had been made by the new authority.

(3) The new authority shall within 6 weeks of the date of the transfer serve a notice on the child's parent informing him–

   (a) that the statement has been transferred;

   (b) whether they propose to make an assessment under section 167; and

   (c) when they propose to review the statement in accordance with paragraph (4).

(4) The new authority shall review the statement under section 172(5) before the expiry of whichever of the following two periods expires later–

   (a) the period of twelve months beginning with the making of the statement, or as the case may be, with the previous review, or

   (b) the period of three months beginning with the date of the transfer.

(5) Where by virtue of the transfer the new authority comes under a duty to arrange the child's attendance at a school specified in the statement but in light of the child's move that attendance is no longer practicable the new authority may arrange for the child's attendance at another school appropri-

ate for the child until such time as it is possible to amend the statement in accordance with paragraph 10 of Schedule 10 to the Act.

RESTRICTION ON DISCLOSURE OF STATEMENTS

19.–(1) Subject to the provisions of the Act and of these Regulations, a statement in respect of a child shall not be disclosed without the parent's consent except–

(a) to persons to whom, in the opinion of the authority concerned, the statement should be disclosed in the educational interests of the child;

(b) for the purposes of any appeal under section 170 of the Act;

(c) for the purposes of educational research which, in the opinion of the authority, may advance the education of children with special educational needs, if, but only if, the person engaged in that research undertakes not to publish anything contained in, or derived from, a statement otherwise than in a form which does not identify any individual concerned including, in particular, the child concerned and his parent;

(d) on the order of any court or for the purposes of any criminal proceedings;

(e) for the purposes of any investigation under Part III of the Local Government Act 1974 (investigation of maladministration)(**h**);

(f) to the Secretary of State when he requests such disclosure for the purposes of deciding whether to give directions or make an order under section 68 or 99 of the Education Act 1944(**i**);

(g) for the purposes of an assessment of the needs of the child with respect to the provision of any statutory services for him being carried out by officers of a social services authority by virtue of arrangements made under section 5(5) of the Disabled Persons (Services, Consultation and Representation) Act 1986(**j**); or

(h) for the purposes of a local authority in the performance of their duties under sections 22(3)(a), 85(4)(a), 86(3)(a) and 87(3) of the Children Act 1989(**k**).

(2) The arrangements for keeping such statements shall be such as to ensure, so far as is reasonably practicable, that unauthorised persons do not have access to them.

(3) In this regulation any reference to a statement includes a reference to any representations, evidence, advice or information which is set out therein in pursuance of regulation 11(1)(d).

Disabled Persons (Services, Consultation and Representation) Act 1986
Extracts

An Act to provide for the improvement of the effectiveness of, and the co-ordination of resources in, the provision of services for people with mental or physical handicap and for people with mental illness; to make further provision for the assessment of the needs of such people; to establish further consultative processes and representational rights for such people; and for connected purposes. [8th July 1986]

Services under s.2 of the 1970 Act: duty to consider needs of disabled persons
4. When requested to do so by–

(a) a disabled person,

(b) his authorised representative, or

(c) any person who provides care for him in the circumstances mentioned in section 8,

a local authority shall decide whether the needs of the disabled person call for the provision by the authority of any services in accordance with section 2(1) of the 1970 Act (provision of welfare services).

Disabled persons leaving special education
5.–(1) Where–

(a) a local education authority have made a statement under section 7 of the Education Act 1981 (statement of child's educational needs) in respect of a child under the age of 14, and

(b) the statement is still maintained by the authority at whichever is the earlier of the following times, namely–

(i) the time when they institute the first annual review of the statement following the child's fourteenth birthday, and

(ii) any time falling after that birthday when they institute a re-assessment of his educational needs,

the authority shall at that time require the appropriate officer to give to the authority his opinion as to whether the child is or is not a disabled person.

(2) Where–

(a) a local education authority make any such statement in respect of a child after he has attained the age of 14, or

(b) a local education authority maintain such statement in respect of a child in whose case the appropriate officer has, in pursuance of subsection (1), given his opinion that the child is not a disabled person, but the authority have become aware of a significant change in the mental or physical condition of the child giving them reason to believe that he may now be a disabled person.

the authority shall, at the time of making the statement or (as the case may be) of becoming aware of that change, require the appropriate officer to give to the authority his opinion as to whether the child is or is not a disabled person.

(3) Where an opinion has in pursuance of subsection (1) or (2) been given in the case of a child that he is a disabled person and it subsequently appears to the responsible authority—

(a) that the child will cease to receive full-time education at school on a particular date and will not subsequently be receiving full-time education at a further education establishment, or

(b) that the child will cease to receive full-time education at such an establishment on a particular date,

and (in either case) that he will be under the age of 19 on the relevant date, the authority shall give to the appropriate officer written notification for the purposes of subsection (5) of the date referred to in paragraph (a) or (b); and any such notification shall be given not later than the relevant date and not earlier than four months before that date.

In this subsection 'the relevant date' means the date falling 8 months before the date referred to in paragraph (a) or (b) above.

(4) If at any time it appears to a local education authority—

(a) that a person has on a particular date ceased to receive full-time education as mentioned in paragraph (a) or (b) of subsection (3) or will cease to do so on a particular date falling less than 8 months after that time, and

(b) that no notification of that date has been given to the appropriate officer under that subsection with respect to that person, but

(c) that, had that or any other authority (as the responsible authority for the time being) been aware of his intentions 8 months or more before that date, they would have been required to give notification of that date under that subsection with respect to him,

that authority shall, as soon as is reasonably practicable, give to the appropriate officer written notification for the purposes of subsection (5) of that date.

(5) When the appropriate officer receives a notification given with respect to any person under subsection (3) or (4), he shall (subject to subsections (6) and (7)) make arrangements for the local authority of which he is an officer to carry out an assessment of the needs of that person with respect to the provision by that authority of any statutory services for that person in accordance with any of the welfare enactments, and any such assessment shall be carried out—

(a) in the case of a notification under subsection (3), not later than the end of the period of 5 months beginning with the date of receipt of the notification, or

(b) in the case of a notification under subsection (4), before the date specified in the notification, if reasonably practicable, and in any event not later than the end of the period referred to in paragraph (a) above.

(6) If–

(a) a notification has been given to the appropriate officer with respect to any person under subsection (3) or (4), but

(b) it subsequently appears to a local education authority that that person will be receiving full-time education (whether at school or at a further education establishment) at a time later than the date specified in the notification,

the authority shall give written notification of the relevant facts to that officer as soon as is reasonably practicable; and on receiving any such notification that officer shall cease to be required under subsection (5) to make arrangements for the assessment of the needs of the person in question (but without prejudice to the operation of that subsection in relation to any further notification given with respect to that person under subsection (3) or (4)).

(7) Nothing in subsection (5) shall require the appropriate officer to make arrangements for the assessment of the needs of a person–

(a) if, having attained the age of 16, he has requested that such arrangements should not be made under that subsection, or

(b) if, being under that age, his parent or guardian has made such a request.

(8) Regulations under paragraph 4 of Schedule 1 to the Education Act 1981 (assessments and statements of special educational needs) may, in relation to the transfer of statements made under section 7 of that Act, make such provision as appears to the Secretary of State to be necessary or expedient in connection with the preceding provisions of this section.

(9) In this section–

'the appropriate officer', in relation to the child or person referred to in the provision of this section in question, means such officer as may be appointed for the purposes of this section by the local authority for the area in which that child or person is for the time being ordinarily resident:

'child' means a person of compulsory school age or a person who has attained that age but not the age of 19 and is registered as a pupil at a school or a further education establishment; and

'the responsible authority'–

(a) in relation to a child at school, means the local education authority who are responsible for the child for the purposes of the Education Act 1981;

(b) in relation to a child at a further education establishment, means the local education authority who were responsible for the child immediately before he ceased to receive full-time education at school;

in each case whether any such opinion as is mentioned in subsection (3) was given to that authority or not;

and other expressions used in this section and in the Education Act 1944 (and not defined in this Act) have the same meaning in this section as in that Act.

(10) This section applies to England and Wales only.

Review of expected leaving dates from full-time education of disabled persons

6.–(1) A local education authority shall for the purposes of section 5 above keep under review the dates when the following children are expected to cease to receive full-time education at school or (as the case may be) at a further education establishment, namely–

(a) children for whom that authority are responsible for the purposes of the Education Act 1981 and in the case of each of whom an opinion has been given in pursuance of subsection (1) or (2) of section 5 above that he is a disabled person (whether it was given to that authority or not); and

(b) children at further education establishments for whom that authority were so responsible immediately before they ceased to receive full-time education at school and in the case of each of whom any such opinion had been given as mentioned in paragraph (a).

(2) Subsection (9) of section 5 shall have effect for the purposes of this section as it has effect for the purposes of that section.

Duty of local authority to take into account abilities of carer

8.–(1) Where–

(a) a disabled person is living at home and receiving a substantial amount of care on a regular basis from another person (who is not a person employed to provide such care by any body in the exercise of its functions under any enactment), and

(b) it falls to a local authority to decide whether the disabled person's needs call for the provision by them of any services for him under any of the welfare enactments,

the local authority shall, in deciding that question, have regard to the ability of that other person to continue to provide such care on a regular basis.

(2) Where that other person is unable to communicate, or (as the case may be) be communicated with, orally or in writing (or in each of those ways) by reason of any mental or physical incapacity, the local authority shall provide such services as, in their opinion, are necessary to ensure that any such incapacity does not prevent the authority from being properly informed as to the ability of that person to continue to provide care as mentioned in subsection (1).

(3) Section 3(7) shall apply for the purposes of subsection (2) above as it applies for the purposes of section 3(6), but as if any reference to the disabled

person or his authorised representative were a reference to the person mentioned in subsection (2).

PART II
INFORMATION AND CONSULTATION

Information

9. In subsection (2)(b) of section 1 of the 1970 Act–

    (a) for the words 'any other of those services' there shall be substituted the words 'any other service provided by the authority (whether under any such arrangements or not)'; and

    (b) at the end there shall be inserted the words 'and of any service provided by any other authority or organisation which in the opinion of the authority is so relevant and of which particulars are in the authority's possession.'.

Co-option to committees etc. of persons representing interests of disabled persons

10. Where any enactment provides for the appointment or co-option to any council, committee or body of one or more persons with special knowledge of the needs of disabled persons, such appointment or co-option shall only be made after consultation with such organisation or organisations of disabled people as may be appropriate in each case.

Circular to Local Authorities, January 1988

DEPARTMENT OF HEALTH AND SOCIAL SECURITY
WELSH OFFICE, DEPARTMENT OF EDUCATION AND SCIENCE

I. SUMMARY

This Circular draws the attention of local authorities, Chief Education Officers and Directors of Social Services to the implementation of sections 5 and 6 of the Disabled Persons (Services, Consultation and Representation) Act 1986 and gives guidance on the effect of those provisions.

II. INTRODUCTION

1. The Secretary of State for Social Services has made an order bringing sections 5 and 6 of the Disabled Persons (Services, Consultation and Representation) Act 1986 into effect on 1 February 1988.

2. The purpose of sections 5 and 6 is to ensure a smooth transition for a disabled child between full-time education and adult life. They aim to achieve this by providing for closer co-operation between the local education authority (LEA) and the Social Services Department (SSD) at two points, first as the child approaches the end of compulsory education, and second in the final year of full-time education.

3. LEAs and SSDs will need to review their procedures to achieve speedy and reliable transfers of information within and between their two departments, and to identify appropriate contact points.

4. Certain terms used in this circular marked with an asterisk, such as 'child', are given the particular meaning that they have in the Act. There is an Annex of definitions at the end of this circular.

III. MAIN PROVISIONS OF SECTIONS

5. **Section 5**: This section refers to children with statements of special educational needs under the Education Act 1981.

  a. Under this section, the responsible local education authority (LEA) is required to seek an opinion from the SSD on whether a child* who is the subject of a statement of special educational needs under section 7 of the Education Act 1981 is a disabled person*.

  b. The SSD is required to provide an opinion to the LEA as to whether the child is or is not a disabled person.

c. The LEA is required, having been notified that a child is a disabled person, to notify the SSD in writing of the date that that child will cease to receive full-time education.

d. The SSD must then make arrangements to carry out an assessment of the needs of that disabled person with respect to the provision of any statutory services for that person in accordance with any of the 'welfare enactments'*.

6. **Section 6**: This section requires LEAs to keep under review the leaving dates from full-time education at school or a further education establishment of children who have been identified as disabled.

IV. DUTIES OF EDUCATION AUTHORITIES

7. The LEA must obtain an opinion as to whether a child is or is not a disabled person as part of the first annual review or assessment or reassessment after the child's 14th birthday. In practice this will take place:

i. as part of the mandatory reassessment of the child's special educational needs carried out when the child is between the ages of 13½ and 14½, if that falls after the 14th birthday; or

ii. as part of the annual review of the child's statement of special educational needs in his 15th year; or

iii. at a later stage in the case of a child over 14 either being assessed for the first time, or whose mental or physical condition has, in the view of the LEA, changed significantly since an opinion was last sought.

LEAs and SSDs will need to act quickly in the case of those children who fall into category 7.iii above, where only a short time remains before the child leaves full-time education.

8. Where an LEA seeks an opinion as to whether a child is disabled, they may wish to inform the family (parent or guardian or the child if he or she is aged 16 or over) that this is being done, and to explain the reasons for it.

V. DUTY OF APPROPRIATE OFFICER TO IDENTIFY A CHILD WHO IS DISABLED

9. It will be necessary for the SSD to appoint an 'appropriate officer*' to give an opinion as to whether any child referred to them by the LEA is or is not a disabled person and to notify the LEA accordingly.

10. When the appropriate officer is asked by the education authority to give an opinion as to whether or not a statemented child is a disabled person, it is important that this is done reasonably promptly. Where personal contact with the child is considered appropriate but the parent or guardian or child (as the case may be) does not cooperate, the appropriate officer will have to base his opinion as to whether or not the child is a disabled person on the information available. Delay in identifying a child as disabled could in turn prevent the LEA notifying the SSD of the expected date that the child will leave school

and thereby restrict the time available for an assessment of welfare needs to be undertaken.

VI. ARRANGEMENTS FOR NOTIFYING DATE OF LEAVING FULL-TIME EDUCATION

11. The LEA will have to notify the appropriate officer of the SSD *not later than 8 months* in advance (the 'relevant date*' in the Act) of the date on which children who have been identified as disabled are expected to leave full-time education, whether school or further education. This must *not* be done, however, *more than 12 months before* the expected leaving date. For children transferring to a part time place in a college of further education, notification must be given not later than 8 months before the child leaves school.

12. LEAs may not be able to state the precise date on which a child is expected to leave full-time education. The Act recognises this difficulty and allows for the procedures set out in paragraph 11 above to be varied in the following circumstances:

a. If a notification has been given to the appropriate officer and the LEA finds out that the leaving date will be postponed or advanced the appropriate officer of the SSD must be notified of this fact as soon as reasonably practicable.

b. Where an LEA finds itself with less than 8 months in which to notify the appropriate officer of the SSD that the child is leaving school, it must take action to notify the appropriate officer of the social services department in writing of the leaving date as soon as possible.

VII. YOUNG PEOPLE IN FULL-TIME EDUCATION AFTER THEIR NINETEENTH BIRTHDAY

13. Some young people who have been identified as disabled stay on beyond their 19th birthday in order to complete a course of full-time education in a school or college of further education. An LEA is not statutorily required to notify the SSD of the date when a disabled young person is expected to leave full-time education if, on the relevant date (ie 8 months before the expected leaving date), the young person is 19 or over. However, where disabled young people have continued in full-time education since the age of 16, it is hoped that authorities will exercise their discretion and accord them the same provision under sections 5 and 6 that they would have enjoyed had they elected to leave full-time education before the age of 19.

Any disabled young person will of course have the right, if he or she so requests, to have his or her needs assessed by virtue of section 4 of this Act, in accordance with section 2(1) of the Chronically Sick and Disabled Persons Act 1970 (See Circular LAC(87)6).

VIII. ARRANGEMENTS TO BE UNDERTAKEN BY THE SSD ONCE THE LEAVING DATE HAS BEEN NOTIFIED

14. On receipt of the written notification from the LEA that a child who has been identified as a disabled person will leave full-time education, the appropriate officer is required to make arrangements for the local authority to carry out an assessment of the needs of the disabled person for the provision of statutory services under any of the welfare enactments. SSDs will need to have regard to the ability of the carer to provide care on a regular basis, where the disabled person is living at home (Section 8(1) of this Act). Apart from assessing the need for the services specifically mentioned in the welfare enactments; and arranging for their provision, local authorities will wish to give such advice as they can about other matters affecting the welfare of the disabled person and his family or carers, and to refer them to other agencies as appropriate. Such advice might cover employment, higher and further education, health care and possible entitlement to social security benefits. The giving of such advice comes within the terms of section 1(2) of the CSDP Act as amended by section 9 of this Act. (See Circular LAC(87)6)

Examples of these services are at Annex 2

IX. TIMETABLE FOR ASSESSMENT

15. The assessment of the needs of the disabled person is required to be carried out according to the following timetable:

a. Where the notification of leaving full-time education has been provided by the relevant date, within 5 months of that date, ie 3 months before leaving full-time education.

b. Where the notification is received by the appropriate officer after the relevant date, (ie less than 8 months before leaving full-time education) before the school-leaving date, if reasonably practicable, and in any event not later than 5 months after receiving the notification.

c. Where notification is given to the appropriate officer that a person's leaving date will be postponed or advanced it is not necessary to make arrangements for an assessment to be carried out until further notification under section 5(3) or 5(4) of the Act is received.

16. The appropriate officer should not make arrangements for an assessment of the disabled person's needs to be undertaken where the parent or guardian (if the child is under 16) or the young person (if he or she is aged 16 or over) requests that this is not carried out.

X. INTERIM ARRANGEMENTS

17. The first group of children to come within the statutory provisions of sections 5 and 6 of the Act following implementation on 1 February 1988 are in the main those who are able to leave school during or at the end of the summer term 1990.

18. The Secretaries of State are anxious to ensure that those disabled children who will not fall within the statutory provision of section 5 of the Act, but who leave full-time education after the implementation date are able to benefit as far as possible from these notification and assessment procedures.

19. With respect to 1989 school leavers, while it will not be possible to follow the timetable for identification, notification and assessment, the Secretaries of State hope that, subject to local circumstances, LEAs and SSDs will endeavour to undertake the functions set out in section 5 of this Act albeit to a shortened timetable for as many children as possible either before they leave full-time education or as soon as practicable thereafter.

20. With respect to 1988 leavers LEAs and SSDs are requested to consider to what extent it may be possible to make some arrangements in respect of individual disabled children of whom they are aware.

Costs
21. The resource implications of the implementation of these sections were considered by the local authority associations who have accepted that allowance for the additional costs arising from sections 5 and 6 in 1988/89, mainly in relation to the identification and assessment of disabled school leavers, has been made in the Personal Social Services provision for that year. The estimated additional service costs arising from assessments made under section 5 in 1989/90 and subsequent years will be taken into account in the public expenditure discussions for the appropriate year.

22. Recipients are asked to bring this Circular to the attention of all staff involved in the provision of services to disabled young people, and in recording details of children with special educational needs.

ANNEX 1 DEFINITIONS OF TERMS USED IN THE CIRCULAR

Appropriate Officer
Section 5(9) of this Act refers to 'such officer as may be appointed for the purposes of this section of the Act by the local authority for the area in which the child or person is for the time being ordinarily resident'. It is for local authorities to determine the arrangements for discharging the tasks of the appropriate officer as set out in this section of the Act. These tasks may be delegated to one or more persons but are carried out in the name of the appropriate officer.

Child
A person of compulsory school age or a person under the age of 19 registered as a pupil of a school or a further education establishment.

Disabled Person
Section 29 of the National Assistance Act 1948 (as amended) applies to:

'persons who are blind, deaf or dumb, or who suffer from mental disorder of any description, and other persons who are substantially and permanently handicapped by illness, injury, or congenital deformity or such other disabilities as may be prescribed by the Minister.'

(No regulations have been made prescribing any other disability)

Ordinarily Resident
In the case of disabled children who have been receiving special education away from their parents' or guardian's home their ordinary residence would normally be that of their parents or guardian.

Relevant Date
The date falling 8 months before a child, identified as disabled, either
> a. will cease to receive full-time education at school, and not subsequently receive full-time education at a further education establishment or
> b. will cease to receive full-time education at a further education establishment.

Social Services Department
(SSD) refers to the local authority for the area in which the child or person is for the time being ordinarily resident (see definition above). Local authority means a council which is a local authority for the purposes of the Local Authority Social Services Act 1970.

Welfare Enactments
Part III of the National Assistance Act 1948
Section 2 of the Chronically Sick and Disabled Persons Act 1970
Schedule 8 of the National Health Service Act 1977.

ANNEX 2 LOCAL AUTHORITY SERVICES

The services which social services departments will need to consider include:
> Social work advice and support
> Facilities for social rehabilitation and adjustment to disability including assistance in overcoming limitations of mobility or communication
> Respite care
> Day care facilities
> Residential accommodation
> Adaptations to premises
> Meals at home
> Practical assistance (including home helps)
> Recreational needs (TV, radio, library facilities etc)
> Laundry needs
> Travel to and from facilities provided for disabled people
> Adult Training Centres/Social Education Centres
> Recreational and educational facilities (including holidays)

Services which a social services department would wish to take into account, although not their direct responsibility:

Educational and vocational training
Health needs in liaison with medical services
Social security
Housing
Employment

Local Authority Circular, March 1993

DEPARTMENT OF HEALTH

I. SUMMARY

This circular draws the attention of Directors of Social Services to changes in the application of Sections 5 and 6 of the Disabled Persons (Services, Consultation and Representation) Act 1986, following the introduction of the Further and Higher Education Act 1992, and gives guidance on the effect of those provisions.

II. INTRODUCTION

1. The Further and Higher Education Act 1992 provides for the establishment of Further Education Funding Councils for England and Wales; transfers to them some of Local Education Authorities' (LEAs) statutory duties to secure the provision of further education; and provides for the transfer of colleges of further education and sixth form colleges from LEA control. The colleges will be incorporated as independent institutions and will be vested with the assets which are held by them immediately before their change in status. The Funding Councils will allocate funds provided by the Secretary of State for Education to institutions in the new further education structure.

2. Sections 5 and 6 of the Disabled Persons (SCR) Act 1986 are concerned with the identification of young disabled people as they leave school and the assessment of their needs for a range of welfare services. A key provision is a requirement for LEAs to notify Social Services Departments (SSDs) of the dates when young people with disabilities are to leave school, so as to trigger the assessment of their needs for welfare services.

3. The removal of further education and Sixth Form Colleges from LEA control means that it will no longer be appropriate for LEAs to be required to notify SSDs of the leaving dates of young disabled people in further education. To assist the transition process from the LEA sector to the FEFC sector and beyond, paragraphs 91 and 92 of Schedule 8 to the new Act make substantial amendments to sections 5 and 6 of the Disabled Persons (SCR) Act 1986, in connection with the notifications necessary when a disabled student reaches, or is over, compulsory school age.

III. RESPONSIBILITY FOR NOTIFYING DATES

4. There is a continuing requirement for LEAs to notify SSDs of the expected date that disabled students will leave school, so that an assessment of welfare

needs can be undertaken, where authorities are responsible for them for the purposes of the Education Act 1981, and to keep under review the date when the individual concerned is expected to cease to receive relevant full-time education. This includes children at a school maintained by the LEA as well as, for example, a grant-maintained school.

5.   When a young person moves into the FEFC sector, the governing body of the relevant educational institution has a duty to notify the SSD of the expected date that the young person will leave full-time education.

6.   The FEFC itself will be required to notify SSDs of a young disabled person's leaving date, if it has arranged provision for that person in an establishment outside the Council's remit, e.g. an independent college.

7.   A further requirement is for LEAs to notify SSDs of the future plans of all disabled young people, when they reach the end of compulsory education – whether leaving, staying on, or moving into the FEFC sector – to assist SSDs in keeping track of the potential need for welfare services.

IV.   COLLABORATION BETWEEN AGENCIES FOR ASSESSING NEEDS

8.   A number of agencies may be involved in providing advice or support for an individual disabled person, including the careers service, health authorities, social services departments and voluntary organisations, and may act on the individual's behalf in articulating demand for further education. The arrangements for assessment should take account of the role of any agencies involved. Inter-agency collaboration is essential, particularly to co-ordinate the contribution of the various services in complex cases and the Secretary of State has invited SSDs to promote such inter-agency cooperation to ensure the best possible response to students needs: [see similar request to the FEFC and LEAs – Section IV, paragraph 74 of the DFE's Circular 1/93 refers].

V.   COSTS

9.   SSDs have been reminded of their duty under Section 2(1)(c) of the Chronically Sick and Disabled Persons Act 1970 to make arrangements for assisting a disabled person who is ordinarily resident in their area in taking advantage of educational facilities available to him/her, (even where provision is made outside that local authority's area), if they are satisfied that it is necessary in order to meet that person's needs. Such assistance might, in appropriate cases, include the funding by the local authority of the personal care required to enable the student in question to pursue his/her studies. It is, of course, for the authority to decide, in each case, what the individual's needs are, and how they are to be met.

10.   Disabled students attending higher education courses may be eligible to receive up to three Disabled Students Allowances from the local education authority, as part of their mandatory award. These allowances are for a non-medical helper, major items of special equipment, or minor items such as

tapes and braille paper. They are aimed at helping students with costs related to their course, and are not intended to meet other costs arising from their disability which would have to be met irrespective of whether or not they were on a course. For those attending further education courses, similar support may be provided at the discretion of the LEA.

11.   There may be occasions where the Social Services Department is asked to consider the provision of additional care support for an individual who will receive a Disabled Students Allowance or discretionary support from the LEA. It will, therefore, be appropriate in some circumstances for support for an individual's personal care needs to be provided jointly by the SSD and the LEA.

VI. FURTHER INFORMATION

12.   This circular should be read in conjunction with LAC(88)2, which is still extant.

Circular
Students with Learning Difficulties and/or Disabilities by the Further Education Funding Council

PART 1 – LEGAL BACKGROUND
Role and Responsibilities of the Council

7 The Further and Higher Education Act 1992 (the Act) places a range of duties upon the Council to secure provision of further education which are:
- sufficient for the needs of full-time students aged 16–18
- adequate for the needs of full-time students aged 19 and over and part-time students aged over 16 where the course of study falls within the scope of schedule 2 of the Act.

8 Schedule 2 to the Act sets out a range of courses which lead to a vocational or other recognised qualification, either directly or indirectly. A copy of schedule 2 is attached at annex A, together with the Council's guidance on interpreting aspects of the schedule. The Council also has the duty, when securing provision of further education, to avoid disproportionate expenditure and to make the most effective use of its resources.

9 When discharging the general duties outlined above, the Council is required under the Act to have regard to the requirements of students with learning difficulties and/or disabilities. The Act states that a person has a learning difficulty if he/she has a significantly greater difficulty in learning than the majority of persons of his/her age; or he/she has a disability which prevents or hinders him/her from making use of facilities of a kind generally provided by colleges within the further education sector for people of his/her age. The Act also states that a person should not be taken to have a learning difficulty solely because the language or form of language in which he/she will be taught is different from that which has at any time been spoken in his/her home.

10 Section 4 of the Act states that the Council shall secure provision at an institution outside the sector for a student with learning difficulties and/or disabilities for whom adequate facilities are not available at an institution in the sector, where this is in the student's best interests. This duty applies to students up to the age of 25. For the purpose of this circular, institutions outside the sector are referred to as specialist colleges outside the sector.

11 The Council's duties under the Act towards students with learning difficulties and/or disabilities and the ways in which these should be dis-

charged have been further outlined in the secretary of state's letter of guidance to the Council, published in Circular 92/08. This asked the Council to ensure that wherever possible, learning difficulties should be no bar to access to further education. The secretary of state also emphasised the importance of assessing a student's educational needs and of inter-agency collaboration in contributing to arrangements that would meet those needs.

12 In the light of these responsibilities, the Council has agreed criteria by which it will find students to attend specialist colleges outside the sector. These are shown at annex B.

Role and Responsibilities of Local Education Authorities

13 The Department for Education (DFE) circular 01/93, issued on 5 January 1993, outlines the continuing responsibilities of LEAs after colleges were given corporate status on 1 April 1993. These responsibilities cover:

- pupils over the age of 16 attending schools
- the provision of transport for students attending courses of further education, where it is considered necessary and in some circumstances
- the power to provide discretionary awards to students in further education.

14 Local authorities also have extensive duties and powers in respect of young people with learning difficulties and/or disabilities under other recent legislation including the Children Act 1989, the Education Act 1981 and the Disabled Persons (Services, Consultation and Representation) Act 1986.

15 LEAs continue to offer considerable expertise and support to young people with learning difficulties and/or disabilities as they reach the end of their compulsory schooling and where they are considering embarking upon further education. Local authorities provide equipment, guidance and advice to young people and their families. They are well placed to offer balanced advice to young people about their educational choices at 16 and beyond. This is often a particular responsibility of the careers service, which retains specific and important duties in areas where the service is provided directly by the local authority as well as those which operate under a pathfinder contract.

16 The Education Act 1993 alters significantly the arrangements which LEAs must put in place for pupils with learning difficulties and/or disabilities who have a statement of special educational need under the Education Act 1981. The arrangements will, from 1 September 1994, include the establishment of a tribunal to consider complaints against LEAs in drawing up a statement and in delivery the appropriate provision for a pupil. They will also place new emphasis on the annual review of a statement, particularly at the age of 14, under the transition plan, and on putting in place arrangements to ensure that pupils can make an effective transition from school to further education. The arrangements required by the Education Act 1993 are set out in a series of draft documents and regulations published for consultation by the DFE over recent months. These are due to be finalised in the spring and summer of 1994.

17 Pupils over 16 years of age who have learning difficulties and/or disabilities are the responsibility of their home LEA not the Council where they have statements of special educational need. This includes pupils whose statements require provision to be made for them in an independent school. As defined in legislation, a school includes an establishment which provides secondary education for children below the statutory school leaving age.

PART 2 – PROVISION FOR STUDENTS AT SPECIALIST COL- LEGES OUTSIDE THE SECTOR

18 The Council has established its arrangements for securing provision for students at specialist colleges outside the sector in the context of the legal background described in part 1 of this circular. The arrangements therefore reflect the respective roles and responsibilities of the Council and LEAs. A formal agreement has been reached between the Council and the local author- ity associations which recognises the important contribution made by local authorities particularly to:

- assessing the educational needs of young people with learning difficulties and/or disabilities
- supporting their effective transition to further education, where that is appropriate.

Assessment of Educational Needs and Recommendations made by LEAs

19 The agreement referred to in paragraph 18 is attached at annex C. The function of the agreement is to yield a thorough assessment of a student's educational needs so that the Council can take appropriate decisions about a student who may require further education provision at a specialist college outside the sector. The assessment will underpin the recommendations made to the Council by the student's home local authority where it considers that, on the basis of the assessment, his/her educational needs cannot be met at a school or sector college. The agreement indicates the agency within the local authority which would normally be expected to originate a recommendation to the Council. As well as informing the Council about a student's educational needs, a thorough assessment is important as a way of helping the student identify his/her preferences and of describing an appropriate further educa- tional learning programme with clear objectives and support needs.

20 Wherever possible, a recommendation should be made only where the student's assessment includes a report of a visit to, or stay at, the student's first choice specialist college shown in the recommendation. The Council expects that specialist colleges will include the cost of assessments within their overall fee structure.

21 Further details of thorough assessments of educational needs are in- cluded at paragraphs 14–16 of the agreement at annex C. Recommendations should be made on the recommendation form for a new student or the recommendation form for an extension included with this guidance at an- nexes E and F.

Scope of the Agreement

22 The agreement between the Council and the Association of County Councils (ACC) and the Association of Metropolitan Authorities (AMA) covers students who wish to attend a specialist college outside the sector:

- for whom the local authority currently has a responsibility
- for whom local sector provision is not adequate
- who come within the scope of the Council's legal duties.

23 Full details are given within the text of the agreement.

24 For students covered by paragraph 13(A) and (c) of the agreement the local authority will usually have a full range of information available on which to base an assessment and recommendation. Most of these students will previously have had a statement of special educational need underpinned in turn by extensive expert information on the student's educational needs.

25 For students covered by paragraph 13(b) and (d) of the agreement, the local authority may have less comprehensive or up-to-date information, although it will probably have some information which could assist a thorough assessment. Where this is the case, the Council will contact the student's local authority to establish the extent of the available information. It may then make arrangements for assessing the student's educational needs on an individual basis. Where a student who needs to go to a specialist college comes to the attention of a college in the sector, a local authority or specialist college outside the sector, the head of the Council's regional office in the area in which the student lives should be contacted in order to identify whether a new assessment of educational needs is required. With the exception of any costs of assessment which are incurred by the specialist college, and which should be incorporated into the fee structure, the Council will, when necessary, be prepared to consider contributing towards the cost of an assessment of such a student's educational needs. Such an assessment will be required to be objective and sufficiently comprehensive to inform the Council's decision. The relevant regional office should be contacted first.

Extended Provision at a Specialist College

26 Some students currently at a specialist college outside the sector on a course which falls within the Council's duties may wish to extend their placement beyond the duration originally agreed, whether by the Council or the student's home local authority. For example the student may wish to have a longer period to complete his/her course or to start a new course. The Council will need to take a decision in each case. To do so, it will require:

- a summary of the progress made by the student
- an assessment of the student's achievements against the original objectives
- a detailed explanation of why the student requires continued provision, indicating, among other things, the new objectives to be achieved and why the proposed provision is in his/her best interests.

27 There is a separate form for recommendations for students seeking an extension at the back of the guidance (annex F). The Council will expect such

recommendations to be made by the local authority but where this is not appropriate it will seek the views of the local authority about the student.

28 It is unlikely that information from the specialist college alone will be sufficient to enable the Council to reach a decision about such students. Attention is drawn to the criteria and factors for consideration by the council in order to reach a decision about extension recommendations, set out in annex B.

Council Considerations

29 In reaching a decision about a recommendation for a new student or about an extension for an existing student, the Council will have regard to:

- its legal duties under the Further and Higher Education Act 1992
- the criteria for decisions and factors to be taken into account.

30 Recommendations received by the Council will be considered by the relevant regional office. The Council's regional offices are steadily building up their knowledge of relevant provision and have, during 1993–94, established positive and effective relationships with staff in local authorities. The Council also has procedures for moderating decisions, in order to ensure consistency and equity.

31 In the light of its legal duties the Council may wish to agree to joint funding for a student for example with the student's social services department, health authority, local education authority or other body. Whilst it is difficult to prescribe in advance the precise circumstances, experience to date and the duties of other agencies indicate that this is likely to apply where:

- the Council considers that the student and/or his/her proposed course of study is partially within the scope of its legal duties
- the reasons for residential education do not arise predominantly from educational needs
- the student is also a client of another agency, for example, having a care plan which includes educational provision as part of an overall package to which other agencies are also contributing
- the student receives social security benefits and allowances which contribute to the total costs of his/her provision.

32 To this end the two recommendation forms include reference to funding from, and the responsibility of, other agencies. The Council would expect that, wherever possible, funding decisions can be taken by the relevant agencies before a form is forwarded to it.

33 The Council's consideration of a recommendation in the light of its legal duties may also lead to it agree a shorter period of funding in the first instance than requested originally.

Communications

34 The Council is committed to ensuring that its funding arrangements and decision-making processes are equitable and easily understood. To this end, it has published its criteria and the factors to be taken in to account when reaching a decision at annex B. It is also sensitive to the need to recognise that

students with learning difficulties and/or disabilities are seeking to attain adult status and independence. The Council is therefore developing a booklet for students setting out the Council's duties and the arrangements which obtain for 1994–95. Copies will be made available to LEAs and specialist colleges. A copy will also be sent to each student about whom a recommendation form is received by the Council.

35 The Council considers that the views of students are central to the choice of post-16 provision and this is reflected in the arrangements set out in the guidance. The Council will wish to be assured that each student for whom a recommendation is received has been fully involved in the assessment of his/her educational needs, supports the recommendation made on his/her behalf and that he/she or his/her family/advocate is content for the information arising from the assessment of educational needs to be made available to the Council. This is reflected in the two forms enclosed with the guidance.

36 For 1994–95 the Council will communicate its decisions to the student, his/her parent/advocate and the referring agency at the same time. Where the Council decides not to fund the student's place, it will explain its reasons in the light of the criteria and factors set out at annex B.

37 Recommendation forms should be photocopied and when completed, forwarded to the appropriate regional office. these are shown at annex D.

Reviews of Decisions

38 Where the student and his/her parent/advocate are not content with the Council's decision they may request that it be reviewed. For 1994–95 the review arrangements will be as follows:

- an invitation to provide additional information which might lead the Council to a different decision. This information should address the considerations shown in annex B. It will be considered by the regional office and a decision communicated to the student and his/her parent/advocate

- where the student and his/her parent/advocate continue to be dissatisfied with the decision they may request that the decision is reviewed by an appeals panel. This panel will comprise independent people from outside the Council's own staff. The panel will be able to commission additional expert advice where necessary.

Payments

39 Where the Council agrees to secure a place for a student at a specialist college outside the sector, fee payments will be made termly on receipt of an invoice on a form provided by the Council. Payments are subject to a general agreement between the Council and specialist colleges, copies of which are available on request. In addition, each student will be the subject of a specific agreement, setting out their course or programme of study, funding period and any progress reports required by the Council. It is important that accurate information is provided about the student's learning programme on the relevant recommendation form so that the specific agreement can be appropriately framed.

40 The Council expects that specialist colleges outside the sector will keep fee increases in line with the general funding conditions which prevail within the sector. for 1994–95 the Council has received an allocation of public funds which anticipates that colleges will meet higher pay costs from efficiency gains and which therefore represents an increase in costs to cover inflation of 1 per cent. This is covered by the general agreement between the Council and the specialist colleges.

Quality of Provision at Specialist Colleges

41 The Council has developed an approach to assessing achievement in specialist colleges derived from its work with sector colleges. It is concerned to ensure that students enjoy further educational provision which is of a good standard and which meets their needs. To this end, it has appointed a small team of specialist inspectors who will visit these colleges and assess the quality of the provision they offer. The approach has been tested during the autumn term 1993. It comprises both the general quality of the educational context within which learning takes place and the individual learning programmes of students funded by the Council. It is possible that the inspectorate's findings will influence future decisions about placements for individual students. Copies of the reports of these visits can be obtained on request from the relevant regional office, once they are available.

Timetable

42 The Council is sensitive to the needs of some students to start their course at different points throughout the year, although the majority will wish to start in September 1994. The Council does not therefore have a closing date for receiving recommendation forms but does require a minimum period in which to give full and proper consideration to those it receives. It would normally expect to reach a decision within six weeks (30 working days) of receipt of a recommendation. The Council has therefore concluded that recommendations received by the beginning of May should be determined by the middle of June, unless additional information or discussion is required. It cannot guarantee that recommendations received after that date or recommendations which do not include adequate information can be determined by the end of the summer term. Early receipt of forms would be welcome.

Enquiries

43 Enquiries about this circular should be directed to the relevant regional office.

ANNEX A: SCHEDULE 2 AND THE COUNCIL'S ASSOCIATED CRITERIA

Type of course/course objective	Criteria for eligibility for funding by FEFC
a. vocational qualification	approved by the secretary of state
b. GCSE or GCE A/AS level GCE/GCSE examining boards	leads to an examination by one of the GCE/GCSE examining boards
c. 'Access' course preparing students for entry to a course of higher education	approved by the secretary of state
d. course which prepared students for entry to courses listed in (a) to (c) above	I. primary course objective is progression to a vocational course GCSE, GCE A/AS level or an Access course as outlined above; and
	ii. course includes accreditation which makes the students eligible to progress to courses (a) to (c); or
	iii. where the course does not include accreditation, evidence of progression to be provided to the Council
e. basic literacy in English	provides students with basic literacy skills
f. teaching English to students where English is not the language spoken at home	improves the knowledge of English for those for whom English is not the language spoken at home
g. basic principles of mathematics	course designed to teach the basic principles of mathematics
h. courses under this part of schedule 2 (courses for proficiency of literacy in Welsh) will be the responsibility of the Welsh Funding Council	I. primary course objective is progression to a course which prepares students for entry to courses listed in sections (a) to (g) above;
	ii. course includes college accreditation which enables the student to progress to courses (d) to (g); or
	iii. evidence of progression to courses (d) to (g) can be provided to the Council.

j. independent living and communication for those with learning difficulties which prepare them for entry to courses (d) to (g).

ANNEX B: FEFC CRITERIA AND FACTORS FOR CONSIDERATION

The Council will take decisions regarding funding for an individual student based on recommendations from local authorities and in the context of its legal duties. Before reaching a decision the Council will consider whether or not the individual and the proposed course of study fall within the scope of those duties. In reaching a decision the Council will take account of the following criteria and factors.

Criteria
- the student's educational needs have been adequately assessed, in particular that the individual and his/her parent/advocate have been involved in the process and that up-to-date professional advice is available

- that the facilities available in the sector are not adequate to meet the individual's needs
- that the recommended placement is in the student's best interests
- that appropriate educational provision cannot be secured for the individual either in the sector or through an alternative placement which would represent better value for money.

Factors

- the qualification/progression aim of the course and the extent to which this meets the educational needs and aspirations of the student
- the additional or specialist learning support required by the student to complete the course
- the arrangements in place for recording and reviewing the student's progress
- the physical suitability of buildings, including residential facilities
- the availability of additional or specialised personal and/or physical support and care arrangements
- opportunities for social and recreational activities
- travelling requirements
- joint funding of the placement with other agencies has been considered in the light of the above criteria
- reasonable account has been taken of the student's expectations of a further education placement
- the schedule 2 content of the course where appropriate
- the likely educational benefits to the student and the costs of the proposed provision.

ANNEX C: AGREEMENT BETWEEN THE FEFC AND THE LOCAL AUTHORITY ASSOCIATIONS

Assessing the educational needs of students with learning difficulties and/or disabilities wishing to attend specialist colleges outside the FEFC sector.

Introduction

1 The purpose of this agreement is to set out formally the respective roles of local authorities and the Further Education Funding Council (the Council) in respect of students with learning difficulties and/or disabilities for whom provision may be secured by the Council at a specialist college outside the further education sector under section 4 of the Further and Higher Education Act 1992 (the Act).

Background

2 Local authorities play a vital part in securing an effective transition for young people with learning difficulties and/or disabilities as defined by the Further and Higher Education Act 1992 from school to further education. This will include, in appropriate circumstances, offering advice about courses, local of study, additional support that may be required, equipment, likely

career opportunities and other aspects relevant to the student's choices at 16 and beyond. The work of local authorities in this context means that they continue to be well placed to assess the educational needs of those students with learning difficulties and/or disabilities for whom further education provision needs to be secured outside the further education sector.

3 The Council has to take decisions about individual students with learning difficulties and/or disabilities on the basis of a thorough assessment of their individual educational needs, in the light of its legal duties.

4 Accordingly, the Council, the Associations of County Councils (ACC) and Association of Metropolitan Authorities (AMA) have reached an agreement which formally recognises the Council's needs and the continuing duties and role of local authorities. This agreement takes account of the role of LEAs following the Further and Higher Education Act 1992 and the Education Act 1993, of social services departments and of the careers service under relevant legislation. The purpose of the agreement with the two associations is to ensure that the best possible advice is given to both individual students and the Council. A code of practice following the Education Act 1993 is currently being considered by the Department for Education. When published, this together with other available guidance and evidence of good practice, will inform the detailed administration which will underpin this agreement.

5 For 1994–95, the agreement has the following components:
- role of local authorities
- role of the Council
- scope of the agreement
- assessment arrangements
- information to be provided to the Council
- communications.

Role of Local Authorities

6 Local authorities are asked for each student who comes within the scope of the agreement and for whom a placement at a specialist college is considered appropriate:
- to make available to the Council advice on the educational needs of the individual student and the supporting assessments carried out by the LEA in meeting its statutory duties, arising particularly under the Education Acts 1981 and 1993
- to identify, in the context of that advice and assessment, where possible, to what extent the required provision and support is unavailable at a sector college
- to recommend to the Council, in the context of that consideration, a placement which will meet the student's needs at an institution outside the sector.

7 In considering the recommendation, the local authority will take account of the student's own views, which will normally be available from their most recent annual review. Under the terms of the Education Act 1993 the student's views will be addressed in the student's transition plan. This provision of the

Act has not yet come into effect but a number of local authorities may be in a position to operate the arrangements earlier.

8 In most cases the appropriate lead agency within the local authority will be the education department. In other cases, the appropriate lead agency will be the careers service. The role of the various agencies within the local authority is set out at paragraphs 12 and 13 below.

Role of the Council

9 The Council's role under this agreement is to:

- receive recommendations in respect of individual students based on an assessment of their educational needs
- reach appropriate decisions about such recommendations against published criteria and in the light of its legal duties
- communicate these decisions appropriately and, wherever possible, in good time.

10 The Council will also play a part in securing effective transition arrangements for individual students; in securing sufficient and adequate facilities for further education; and in continuing to work with local authorities to these ends, within the context of its legal duties.

11 It is also necessary to make arrangements for those few cases where tan LEA does not wish to make a recommendation for a student to attend a specialist college outside the sector and is challenged by the student and/or his/her parent/advocate. The Council will discuss the arrangements for these few cases with the associations in due course. Where a student challenges the Council's decision upon a recommendation received from the student's local authority, the Council's review procedures will apply. These will be explained to the student appropriately.

Scope of the Agreement

12 The agreement between the Council, the ACC and AMA extends to students wishing to attend a specialist college outside the FEFC sector for whom the local authority currently has a responsibility, for whom no sector provision is appropriate, and who come within the scope of the Council's legal duties. The agreement will apply largely to students whose educational needs were previously covered by a statement under the Education Acts 1981 or 1993. In some exceptional cases it will also apply to students whose educational needs are not covered by a statement, but whose educational needs nevertheless require provision to be secured for them at a specialist college outside the sector, where this is the recommendation of the student's local authority.

13 The scope of the agreement and the role of local authority agencies is as follows:

- students rising 16 or otherwise approaching the end of their schooling; recommendations to be received from their home LEA
- older students and/or those who have had a break from education; recommendations to be received from their home LEA if possible. In other cases it might come from another agency within the authority and

the Council might reasonably seek advice or information from the LEA and/or commission an independent assessment of the student's educational needs

- students already attending specialist colleges outside the sector and currently supported by an LEA; recommendations to be received from their home LEA

- students already attending specialist colleges outside the sector and originally placed by the Council; the Council might reasonably seek the views of the student's local authority social services department and/or the careers service. The LEA might be able to confirm historic information, or provide professional expertise if this was specifically invited.

Assessment Arrangements

14 In accordance with recognised best practice, the Council, the ACC and AMA consider that a thorough assessment of a student's educational needs will be based on:

- the young person and his/her parent/advocate receiving a full range of advice and information from the LEA regarding post 16 education and training choices, to inform his/her decision, as indicated in the parent's charter and charter for further education. The careers service has a particular set of responsibilities towards such students in this context and will often take the lead in offering advice and information

- the involvement of the young person, his/her parent/advocate in the assessment process

- the advice, wherever possible, of a range of professionals to ensure expert guidance and a thorough knowledge of the student's educational needs and how these might best be met. These professionals might include educational psychologists; specialist or other careers officers; or other specialist professionals with expert knowledge who have worked with the student during his/her earlier education.

15 Where the student has previously been subject to a statement of special educational needs under the Education Act 1981, it is likely that there will be extensive information available to the local education authority about the student's educational needs and how these can best be met. This information should become increasingly comprehensive and systematic under the terms of the Education Act 1993. In any exceptional cases where a student has not had a statement, it is possible that the information readily available to the local authority will be less extensive. Nonetheless, in order to reach a decision, the Council will need a thorough assessment to be made in order that it can take a soundly-based decision in respect of that individual student. In certain circumstances, the Council may be prepared to commission additional information to supplement any information available from the local authority.

16 The Council expects that arrangements made by specialist colleges outside the sector to assess whether they can appropriately provide for students wishing to attend them will be managed, as currently, by the special-

ist college. Wherever possible, it would not expect a recommendation to be received or determined where the student has not visited the specialist college and had their educational needs assessed.

Information to be Provided to the Council

17 The Council and the local authority associations are aware of the need to ensure confidentiality of information and the student's views and, where appropriate, those of his/her parent/advocate must be sought before the information is offered to the Council. This can be particularly important where the recommendation arising from the assessment of educational need involves information being passed on from a previous phase in the student's education.

18 Local authorities are asked to collate information relating to students with learning difficulties and/or disabilities who requires provision to be secured at a specialist college outside the further education sector to meet their particular educational needs. The information should be drawn from statutory assessments prepared under the Education Acts 1981 and 1993; a transition plan, reviews of the student's progress; records of achievement; as well as advice from the careers service, teachers, and others who have worked with the young person. For a decision about its funding, the Council wishes the information provided to be only that which is relevant to the student's educational needs, although in cases where joint funding may be appropriate, medical or other information may also be necessary to inform a full decision.

19 The subsequent recommendation to the Council should include information about the student; their learning difficulty and/or disability; the resultant educational needs; the appropriate course and specialist college; and comments from the LEA.

20 Under the agreement, for students described in paragraphs 13(a) and (c) local authorities are asked to attach to the recommendation the following documents. Where students are described in paragraphs 13(b) and (d), local authorities are asked to attach as many as possible of the following documents where they are available

- a report from the student's current or most recent school
- a report from an educational psychologist who has worked with the student
- a report from the specialist, or other, careers officer who has worked with the student
- the assessment report from the specialist college at which a placement is recommended.

Communications

21 The Council will inform the student, his/her parent/advocate, the local authority and the recommended specialist college of the outcome of its consideration. Where the Council does not agree to secure the recommended provision reference will be made to the relevant criteria.

Appendix 9

Charities and Voluntary Associations

In the first part of this section organisations offering general help and advice are given. In part two are the societies catering for specific disabilities.

GENERAL

Advisory Centre for Education (ACE)
Unit 1B Aberdeen Studios
22–24 Highbury Grove
London N5 2EA
(0171 354 8321)

Centre for Studies on Inclusive Education (CSIE)
1 Redland Close, Elm Lane
Redland
Bristol BS6 6UE
(0117 923 8450)

The Childrens Society
Edward Rudolph House
Margery Street
London WC1X OJL
(0171 837 4299)

Contact-a-Family
170 Tottenham Court Road
London W1P 0HA
(0171 383 3555)
Publishes a loose-leaf medical directory of Advice and Support Groups for specific conditions.

DIAL UK
Park Lodge, St Catherine's Hospital
Tickhill Road
Doncaster DN4 8QN
(01302 310123)

Disability Alliance
1st Floor East, Universal House
88–94 Wentworth Street
London E1 7SA
(0171 247 8763)

Disability Law Service (Network)
Room 241 2nd Floor
49–51 Bedford Row
London WC1R 4LR
(0171 831 8031)
(Advice service)

Family Fund
Joseph Rowntree Memorial Trust
PO BOX 50
York YO1 1UY
(01904 621115)
Information and advice about educating children with special needs within ordinary schools.

Greater London Association For Disabled People (GLAD)
336 Brixton Road
London SW9 7AA
(0171 274 0107)

I CAN
Barbican City Gate
1–3 Dufferin Street
London EC1Y 8NA
(0171 374 4422)
I CAN is a children's charity for children with speech and language disorders and sufferers of asthma and eczema.

In Touch
10 Norman Road
Sale
Cheshire M33 3DF
(0161 905 2440)
(information and contacts for rare handicapping conditions)

IPSEA (Independent Panel for Special Education Advice)
22 Warren Hill Road
Woodbridge
Suffolk IP12 4DU
(01394 382814)
Consists of independent experts who give advice to parents.

MIND (National Association for Mental Health)
Granta House
15–19 Broadway
Stratford
London E15 4BQ
(0181 519 2122)

National Association of Toy and
Leisure Libraries
68 Churchway
London NW1 1LT
(0171 387 9592)

National Library for the
Handicapped Child
Wellington House
Wellington Road
Wokingham
Berks RG11 1XS
(01734 89110)

National Portage Association
4 Clifton Road
Winchester, Hants
(01962 860148)
(Work with parents of young
handicapped children)

Physically Handicapped and Able
Bodied (PHAB)
12–14 London Road
Croydon
Surrey CRO 2TA
(0181 667 9443)

Pre-school Playgroup Association
61–63 Kings Cross Road
London WC1X 9LL
(0171 833 0991)

Royal Association for Disability and
Rehabilitation (RADAR)
12 City Forum
250 City Road
.London EC1V 8AF
(0171 250 3222)

Royal Society for Mentally
Handicapped Children and Adults
(MENCAP)
123 Golden Lane
London EC1Y ORT
(0171 454 0454)
MENCAP London Division Early Years
project 115 Golden Lane, London EC1Y
OTJ publishes INTERLINK: a London
directory of services for families and
their young children with special
needs.

National Council for Voluntary
Organisations (NCVO)
Regents Wharf, 8 All Saints Street
London N1 9RL
(0171 713 6161)

Young Minds
22a Boston Place
London NW1 6ER
(0171 724 7262)

SOCIETIES CATERING FOR SPECIFIC CONDITIONS
AIDS
National Aids Helplines Call freephone (0800 567 123) 24 hour personal
advice and discussion. Call freephone
(0800 555 777) for National helpline
publicity pack, free leaflets and book-
lets, and an up-to-date list of literature.

Asthma
The National Asthma Campaign
Providence House. Providence Place
London N1 ONT
(0171 226 2260)

Ataxia
Ataxia
Copse Edge
Thursley Road
Elstead, Godlaming
Surrey GU8 6DJ
(01252 702864)

Autism
National Autistic Society
276 Willesden Lane
London NW2 5RB
(0181 451 1114)

Blind and partially sighted
National Federation of the Blind of
the UK
Unity House
Smyth Street
Westgate, Wakefield
W Yorkshire WF1 1ER
(01924 291313)
National Federation of Families with
Visually Impaired Children (LOOK)

Judith Gilboy
The National Office
Queen Alexandra College
49 Court Oak Road
Birmingham B17 9TG
(0121 428 5038)
Facilitates parents' groups and parents
enhancing the education, welfare and

leisure opportunities of visually impaired children.

Royal National Institute for The Blind
224 Great Portland Street
London W1N 6AA
(0171 388 1266)

Bone-marrow disease,
The Anthony Nolan Bone Marrow Trust
Unit 2
Heathgate Buildings
75–87 Agincourt Road
London NW3 2NT
(0171 284 1234)

Brain Damage
Association for Brain-Damaged
Children
Clifton House
3 St Paul's Road
Foleshill
Coventry CV6 5DE
(01203 665450)

Brittle Bones
Brittle Bones Society
Ward 8, Strathmartine Hospital
Strathmartine
DD3 OPG
(01382 667603)

Cerebral Palsy
The Spastics Society
12 Park Crescent
London W1N 4EQ
(0171 636 5020/0800 626216)

Scottish Council for Spastics
11 Corstophine Road
Edinburgh EH12 6HP
(0131 337 9876)

Chest and Heart
The Stroke Association,
CHSA House, White Cross Street
London EC1Y 8JJ
(0171 490 7999)

Clumsiness
Dyspraxia Trust
8 West Alley
Hitchin
Hertfordshire SG5 1EG
(01462 454986)

Colitis and Crohn's
National Association for Colitis and
Crohn's Disease
PO Box 205
St Albans
Hertfordshire AL1 1AB
(01727 844296)

Cystic Fibrosis
Cystic Fibrosis Research Trust
5 Blyth Road
Bromley
Kent BR1 3RS
(0181 464 7211)

Deafness
Breakthrough Trust
Charles W Gillett Centre
998 Bristol Road
Selly Oak
Birmingham B29 6LE
(0121 472 6447)
London Office (0181 853 5661)

British Deaf Association
38 Victoria Place
Carlisle CA1 1HV
(01228 48844)

National Aural Group (NAG),
18 Kings Avenue,
Marcham, Abingdon,
Oxon OX13 6QA
(01865 391492)
A nationwide group of teachers and
parents of deaf children providing
wide-ranging support, information
and advice to help parents help their
deaf children.

National Deaf Children's Society,
45 Hereford Road
London W2 5AH
(0171 229 9272)

Royal National Institute For The Deaf
105 Gower Street
London WC1E 6AH
(0171 387 8033)

Friends for the Young Deaf
FYD Communication Centre
East Court Mansion
Council Offices, College Lane
East Grinstead
West Sussex
(01342 323444)

Deaf/Blind
National Deaf/Blind and Rubella
Association (SENSE)
11–13 Clifton Terrace
Finsbury Park, London N4 3SR
(0171 272 7774)

Diabetes
British Diabetic Association,
10 Queen Anne Street
London W1M 0BD
(0171 323 1531)

Down's Syndrome
Down's Syndrome Association
155 Mitcham Road
London SW17 9PG
(0181 682 4001)

Dyslexia
British Dyslexia Association
98 London Road
Reading, Berkshire RG1 5AU
(01734 668271)

Dyslexia Institute
152 Buckingham Palace Road
London SW1W 9TR
(071 730 8890)

Eczema
National Eczema Society
4 Tavistock Place
London W1CH 9RA
(0171 388 4097)

Epilepsy
Epilepsy Helpline
0800 309030

British Epilepsy Association
Anstey House, 40 Hanover Square
Leeds LS3 1BE
(0113 243 9390)

Epilepsy Association of Scotland
48 Govan Road
Glasgow G51 1JL
(0141 427 4911)

Fragile X Syndrome
Fragile X Society, Mrs Lesley Walker
53 Winchelsea Lane
Hastings
East Sussex TN35 4LG
(01424 81347)

Haemophilia
Haemophilia Society
123 Westminster Bridge Road
London SE1 7HR
(0171 928 2020)

Huntingdon's Disease
Huntingdon's Disease Association
108 Battersea High Street
London SW1 3HP
(0171 223 7000)

Hyperactivity
Hyperactive Children's Support Group
71 Whyke Lane
Chichester
Sussex PO19 2LD
(01903 725182)

Leukaemia
Leukaemia Care Society
14 Kingfisher Court
Venny Bridge, Pinhoe
Exeter
Devon EX4 8JN
(01392 464848)

ME (Myalgic Encephalomyelitis)
ME Association
Stanhope House
High Street
Stanford-le-Hope
Essex SS17 0HA
(01375 642466)

ME Action Campaign
PO Box 1302
Wells
Somerset BA5 2NE
(01749 670799)

Meningitis
National Meningitis Trust
Fern House
Bath Road
Stroud
Gloucestershire GL5 3TJ
(01453 751738)

Mental Impairment
MENCAP (Royal Society for Mentally
Handicapped Children and Adults)
123 Golden Lane
London EC1Y 0RT
(0171 454 0454)

Rathbone Society
1st Floor
Princess House
105–107 Princess Street
Manchester M25 5TU
(0161 236 5358)

Scottish Society for the Mentally
Handicapped
7 Buchanan Street
Glasgow G1 3HL
(0141 226 4541)

Motability
Motability
Gate House, West Gate
The High
Harlow
Essex CM10 1HR
(01279 635666)

Multiple Sclerosis
Federation of MS Therapy Centres
Unit 4
Murdock Road
Bedford MK41 7PD
(01234 325781)

Multiple Scelerosis Society of GB and
Northern Ireland
25 Effie Road
London SW6 1EE
(0171 736 6267)

Muscular Dystrophy
Muscular Dystrophy Group of GB
7–11 Prescott Place
London SW4 6BS
(0171 720 8055)

Physical Disability
Handicapped Adventure Playground
Association
Fulham Palace
Bishops Avenue
London SW6 6EA
(0171 736 4443)

RADAR (Royal Association for
Disablement and Rehabilitation)
12 City Forum
250 City Road
London EC1V 8AF
(0171 250 3222)

REACH (Arm and hand deficient)
Mrs Sue Stokes
12 Wilson Way
Earls Barton
Northants NN6 ONZ
(01604 811041)

STEPS (Leg deficient)
15 Statham Close
Lymm
Cheshire WA13 9NN
(01925 757525)

Spinal Injuries Association
Newport House, 76 St James Lane
London N10 3DF
(0181 444 2121)
A self-help group for children and
adults with spinal cord children.

Prader-Willi Syndrome
Prader-Willi Syndrome Association
30 Follet Drive, Abbots Langley
Herts WD5 OLP
(01923 674543)

Restricted Growth
Restricted Growth Association
PO Box 18, Rugeley
Staffordshire
WS15 2GH
(01889 576571)

Child Growth Foundation
2 Mayfield Avenue
London W4 1PW
(0181 994 7625)

Retinitis Pigmentosa
British Retinis Pigmentosa Society (RPS)
PO Box 350
Buckingham MK18 5EL
(01280 860363)

Rett Syndrome
Rett Syndrome's Association UK
Christine Freeman
29 Carlton Road
London N11 3EX
(0181 361 5161)

Sickle Cell Anaemia
Sickle Cell Society
54 Station Road
London NW10 4UA
(0181 961 7795)

Speech and Language Disorders
AFASIC (Association for all Speech
Impaired Children)
347 Central Markets
London EC1 9NH
(0171 236 3632)

Spina Bifida and Hydrocephalus
Association for Spina Bifida and
Hydrocephalus
Asbah House, 42 Park Road
Peterborough
Cambs PE1 2UQ
(01733 555988)

Spinal Injuries
Spinal Injuries Association
Newport House, 76 St James Lane
London N10 3DF
(0181 444 2121)

Tuberous Sclerosis
Tuberous Sclerosis Association of GB
Mrs Janet Medcalf
Little Barnsley Farm, Milton Road
Catshill, Bromsgrove, Worcs
(01527 871898)

Vaccine Damage
Association of Parents of Vaccine
Damaged Children
Mrs R Fox
2 Church Street
Shipston-on-Stour
Warwickshire CV36 4AP
(01608 661595)

Self Help
More and more areas have their own
self help groups run by and for handicapped people and their parents, who
may produce their own local guides to
services and run advice centres. If there
is one in your area you should be able
to get the address from the Social Services, the local council of Voluntary Services or the local press.

Contact-a-Family
170 Tottenham Court Road
London W1P 0HA
(0171 383 3555)
Has links with over 9000 independant
self help/mutual support groups and
contacts throughout the country. Offers

support and advice to existing groups,
and to parents and professional workers who wish to start a group in their
neighbourhood.

Independent Special Educational
Needs Resource Centre and Helpline
Rosie Johnson
112 Grove Park
Knutsford
Cheshire WA16 8QD
(01565 632666)

Network 81
Co-ordinator – Penny Platt
1–7 Woodfield Terrace
Stanstead
Essex CM24 8AJ
(01279 647415)
A national network of support groups
of parents of children who have special
educational needs.

Parents in Partnership (PiP)
Unit 2
Ground Floor
70 South Lambeth Road
London SW8 1RL
(0171 735 7735)
Assistance to parents of children with
special educational needs with the
statementing procedures under the
education act 1981. Operates in the
Greater London area.

Computer Assistance
ACE (Aids to Communication in
Education)
Ormerod School, Waynflete Road
Headington
Oxford OX3 8DD
(01865 63508)
Assesses children with communic-
ation and learning difficulties.

ACE Access Centre
1 Broadbent Road
Watersheddings, Oldham
Lancashire OL1 4HU
(0161 627 1358)

CENMAC (Centre for Micro-assisted
Communication)
Charlton Park School
Charlton Park Road
London SE7 8HX
(0181 316 7589)

Assesses children and young people with communication difficulties resulting from motor impairment.

National Access Centre, Hereward College of Further Education
Bramston Crescent
Tile Hill Lane
Coventry CV4 9SW
(01203 461231)

Equipment

Disabled Living Foundation
380–384 Harrow Road
London W9 2HU
(0171 289 6111)
Permanent exhibition of aids and information service of many aspects of life for disabled people. By appointment only.

Educational Organisations

Campaign for State Education (CASE)
Secretary
158 Durham Road
London SW20 ODG
(0181 944 8206)
A pressure group of parents seeking to improve the state education system for all.

Centre for Studies on Inclusive Education
1 Redland Close
Elm Lane
Redland
Bristol BS6 6UE
(0117 923 8450)

National Association for the Education of Sick Children
Open School
18 Victoria Park Square
London E2 9PF
(0181 980 6263)

National Association for Special Educational Needs (NASEN)
Central Office
York House, Exhall Grange
Wheelwright Lane
Coventry CV7 9HP
(01203 362414)
An amalgamation of National Association for Remedial Education and National Council for Special Education.

Special Education Consortium
c/o Council for Disabled Children
8 Wakley Street
London EC1V 7QE
(0171 843 6000)

Leisure and Holidays

Local authority social services departments, voluntary societies and schools may also provide leisure activities for handicapped children and young people. Most national organisations for sport and leisure activities, and national youth organisations also make special provisions for handicapped participants.

British Sports Association for the Disabled
Solecroft House
13–27 Brunswick Place
London N1 6DX
(0171 490 4919)

PHAB (Physically Handicapped and Able Bodied) Clubs (including holidays)
12–14 London Road
Croydon
Surrey CRO 2JA
(0181 667 9443)

National Federation of Gateway Clubs (sponsored by MENCAP)
123 Golden Lane
London EC1Y ORT
(0171 454 0454)

Riding for the Disabled Association
National Agricultural Centre
Kenilworth
Warks CV8 2LY
(01203 696510)

Further Education

The National Bureau for Students with Disabilities (SKILL)
336 Brixton Road
London SW9 7AA
(0171 274 0565)
Provides help and advice on further and higher education
(Nationwide telephone information and advice services)

Government Departments and Other Official Bodies

GOVERNMENT DEPARTMENTS AND OTHER OFFICIAL BODIES

Specific enquiries on special education should be addressed to: **Special Education Division,** Department of Education, Sanctuary Buildings, Great Smith Street, London SW1P 3BT (0171 925 5000).

WHERE TO FIND OUT MORE

Department of Education (DOE), Sanctuary Buildings, Great Smith Street, London SW1P 3BT (0171 925 5000).

Welsh Office, Education Department, Phase 2, Government Buildings, Ty Glas Road, Llanishen, Cardiff CF4 5NE (01222 761 456).

Department of Health (DOH), Skipton House, 80 London Road, London SE1 6LW (0171 210 3000).

Council on Tribunals, 22 Kingsway, London WC2B 6LE (0171 936 7045).

Equal Opportunities Commission (EOC), Overseas House, Quay Street, Manchester M3 3HN (0161 833 9244).

Commission for Racial Equality (CRE), Elliot House, 10/12 Allington Street, London SW1E 5EH (0171 828 7022).

Children's Legal Centre, 20 Compton Terrace, London N1 2UN (0171 359 6251).

Independent Panel of Special Educational Advisers (IPSEA), 22 Warren Hill Road, Woodbridge, Suffolk IP12 4DU (01394 382814).

Law Centres Federation, Duchess House, 18 Warren Street, London W1P 5DB (0171 387 8570).

Centre for Studies on Integration in Education (CSIE), 1 Redland Close Elm Lane, Redland, Bristol BS6 6UE (0117 923 8450).